Weights, Measures, and Servings

Abbreviations
Teaspoon – tsp
Tablespoon – tbsp
Gram – g
Ounce – oz
Pound – lb
Kilogram – kg
Litre – ltr
Millilitre – ml
Pint – pt
Fluid ounce – fl oz

Temperature Conversions
Degrees Celsius – °C
Degrees Fahrenheit – °F
120C = 250F = Gas mark 1
150C = 300F = Gas mark 2
160C = 325F = Gas mark 3
180C = 350F = Gas mark 4
200C = 400F = Gas mark 5
220C = 450F = Gas mark 6
240C = 500F = Gas mark 7

Standards Solids

Imperial	Metric
1 oz	30g
2 oz	60g
3 oz	90g
4 oz	125g
5 oz	150g
6 oz	180g
7 oz	200g
8 oz	250g
9 oz	280g
10 oz	310g
11 oz	340g
12 oz	375g
16 oz	500g or 1lb
32 oz	1kg or 2lb

Standards Liquids

Imperial	Metric
1 fl oz	30 ml
2 fl oz	60 ml
3 fl oz	90 ml
4 fl oz	125 ml
5 fl oz	150 ml
6 fl oz	180 ml
7 fl oz	200 ml
8 fl oz	250 ml
9 fl oz	280 ml
(289 ml = ½ pt)	
10 fl oz	310 ml
11 fl oz	340 ml
12 fl oz	375 ml
16 fl oz	500 ml
(568 ml = 1 pt)	
32 fl oz	1 ltr

Author's introduction

SCOTLAND hasn't always had the best of
reputations when it comes to food, despite the
quality of the produce at our disposal.
Our fish, shellfish, beef, venison, lamb, and game are
some of the finest in the world. Along with whisky,
Scotland's food exports are a mainstay of our economy
– but what we have chosen to do with it in the past
hasn't always been something to shout about.

The negative stereotypes of traditional Scottish fayre
are rife, but thankfully we are no longer simply a deep
fried nation, boasting a food revolution we can be
proud of. The fruits of that revolution are evident in
Glasgow and the West, and this guide is a chance to
showcase some of the best we have to offer.

Here, the story of how we have moved away from
that negative reputation is brought to life by those who
have driven through revolution and change. Interviews
and recipes from some of the best known chefs,
restaurateurs and food ambassadors highlight the
journey taken to improve the food scene in Glasgow
and the West.

This new scene is also brought to life by prevalent
'Foodies" – those with a deep, social interest in
food and drink. With an online armoury including
Facebook, Twitter, Instagram, YouTube, and Flickr,
the importance of food bloggers cannot be overlooked,
as they share an instant, widely accessible, critique of
their dining experience from mobile phones and blogs.

Indeed, social media is now widely used by
restaurateurs, who interact with keyboard Foodies',
helping to improve what restaurants are doing. It is
only right then this book offers those same Foodies'
a voice.

To everyone that has taken the time to help and
contribute to this, as well as offer support, I am
eternally grateful. Slanj.

Fraser Wilson

Some hae meat and canna eat,
And some wad eat that want it,
But we hae meat and we can eat,
And sae the Lord be thankit.

Rabbie Burns

First published 2014 by FNW Media
ISBN 978-0-9928982-0-5
Copyright © FNW Media 2014
Introduction copyright © FNW Media 2014
The right of FNW Media to be identified as the author of
this work has been asserted in accordance with the Copyright,
Design, and Patents Act 1988.
Designed by Studio 24 Graphics.
Printed and bound by Free Press Commercial Print.

St Andrew Street
Stranraer
Wigtownshire
DG9 7EB

E: studio24graphics@gmail.com
 www.facebook.com/studio24graphics

Contents

Fáilte

Chief Executive of Scotland Food and Drink, James Withers believes the food scene in Glasgow and the West has blossomed in recent years. So, what's next in this luscious, vibrant part of Scotland?

THE food scene in Scotland as a whole is thriving at the moment, but the West Coast in particular is going through somewhat of a food revolution. More and more people are looking to buy local food - food they can trace. They care more about their food and that interest means we have a thriving industry and food scene.

"There are a number of reasons why it has improved over the last 15-20 years, but by no means is it mission accomplished. There are a lot of areas we need to improve, stemming from people's attitudes towards food and the relatively poor diet we have.

"We are definitely going in the right direction. If you look at menus in restaurants these days, you won't just see steak and chips as an option. You'll see a description of the meat, where it came from, how long it's been hung, the cut. It's the same with everything, seafood, pork - even vegetables.

"This is a truly exciting time for Scotland and we have an opportunity and a platform to leave a lasting impression on people visiting this amazing country about the quality of our food. Tourism is increasing the demand for Scottish food and a massive amount is being spent by tourists when they're visiting - the industry can benefit from it massively.

"This also allows us to showcase the limitless opportunities of food and drink in Scotland. People will walk away from this knowing we have some of the best produce in the world. I'm excited to think we can influence a new generation of people to go home and think about trying Scottish recipes, sourcing Scottish produce, making it a cuisine people want to be a part of."

SCOTLAND
OF FOOD & DRINK

Glasgow

Owner of the Two Fat Ladies and Scottish Fishmonger, Ryan James has been Chairman of the Glasgow Restaurant Association since December 2009, putting him in the ideal position to comment on the food scene in Glasgow, and whether Michelin Star dining fits in.

THE food scene is really buoyant at the moment and there is no shortage of good places opening up. The future looks bright as well and there's going to be many branded, well-known restaurants wanting to get in on the action. Any big name restaurants like Jamie's Italian and the Hard Rock Cafe coming here is a good thing.

"It brings people to the city centre, and if you go on spec and can't get in, you're going to try other restaurants nearby.

"Glasgow is changing as a tourist destination, we are a European hotspot and being more European and 'touristy' has been the biggest change. You could say it started back in 1990 with the Garden Festival, culminating in the Commonwealth Games as the zenith point of that.

"The Merchant City has a number of restaurants that have benefited from tourism, such as Urban, Café Gandolfi, and the Italian Kitchen, all of whom are excellent at what they do.

"There are five Michelin Star restaurants in Edinburgh, but none in Glasgow – people come here for many reasons, but not for that – if they want that, they have to go to Edinburgh. But I don't think there are any places in Glasgow chasing it. Restaurateurs are very nervous of putting their hopes in the Michelin chase. It involves a lot of cash, but in the next two-to-three years there will definitely be a Michelin Star restaurant in Glasgow, which will have a big impact on the scene."

Braised Scotch beef cheek, with roast Jerusalem artichokes

15

176 West Regent Street
Glasgow G2 4RL
T: 0141 248 3801

- 4 x Beef cheeks
- 1 x Carrot
- 2 x Onions
- 1 x Garlic head
- 1 Stick of celery
- 1 Sprig of thyme
- 2ltr Beef stock
- Butter
- Red wine reduction

- 6-8 Jerusalem artichokes
- 50g Parsley
- 50g Rock salt
- 100ml White wine vinegar
- 4 Banana shallots
- 1x Tablespoon sugar
- 1 Pack of wild mushrooms
- Duck fat

Starting with the beef cheeks. Make sure all fat and sinews are off, then cut into three even sized pieces. Heat a large pot separately. Season cheeks and fry really well, ensuring a good colour all over.
While beef is in the pan, peel onions and carrots, chop roughly – same with celery. Cut garlic in half. Take beef out pan and put into a pot, add thyme and stock. Bring to boil, put greaseproof paper or tin foil on top, put in oven at 150°C for 2 – 2 ½ hours. When cooked through, take beef out of stock, then pass stock through a fine sieve. Put back onto reduce, adding red wine reduction; reduce and season.
Peel artichokes, putting into white wine vinegar, with salt and a little water. Put a pot of boiling water on and take artichokes out of vinegar and put into the pot of boiling water. Once water comes back to the

boil, check seasoning then add salt to taste.
Cook for roughly five minutes. When cooked take out, fry lightly in olive oil and a little butter, giving them a nice golden colour. Chop parsley and add to artichokes just before serving.
Peel shallots, put into duck fat and cook slowly for about an hour. When cooked take out of duck fat, then fry all over until a nice golden colour.
Cut wild mushrooms into even sized pieces, wash, fry lightly in olive oil, season to taste.
When reheating beef cheeks, put in a small pan with a little sauce. Place in oven glazing the beef all over, getting a nice even shine on the cheeks.
To plate, put cheeks on plate, artichokes in a heap with mushrooms on top and shallots at the side. Sauce over.

Le Chardon d'Or has been the leading light of Glasgow's restaurant scene since opening. That success comes from the Michelin Star training and experiences of head chef and proprietor, Brian Maule, which resonate with customers the second they step inside. Trained at the hands of the Roux brothers, Brian became the head chef of their world famous Le Gavroche in London before opening the doors to his Glasgow restaurant in 2001.

SCOTLAND is incredibly lucky with the larder we have and as a chef it's a privilege to be able to cook with the best beef, lamb, and fish there is. But we have to make the most of those opportunities.

"During the game season for instance, the produce we get is fantastic and it's really exciting to have the opportunity to cook with wild game.

"It's important that we all respect the produce with the work put in by individuals by providing us with these quality ingredients.

"To ensure quality by pushing for consistency in the kitchen and in the restaurant, we are always looking for feedback to make my business stronger. It's important to us we keep on top of comments, as it makes a big difference in the level of quality we are providing.

"I want people to see that we're professional, friendly and efficient, without being intrusive. It's all about quality and consistency on a daily basis."

R OMAN for the 'one who reigns,' Regent is an appropriate title and street name for Le Chardon d'Or, which has reigned supreme at the hands of Brian Maule since opening.

Situated on Glasgow's West Regent Street, the stunning surroundings of the restaurant give an early indication of what to expect from this fine dining experience. True silver service, glasses gleam, the linen is crisp and spotless, and the food is stunning.

Having headed up the world famous La Gavroche in London for 11 years, Brian Maule turned his attention to opening his own dining experience and quickly set about establishing one of Glasgow's best restaurants.

Diners can expect dishes from a classically French trained chef, but will be blown away by the inspiration and ingenuity that can only be found at the hands of someone trained by the best Michelin Starred chefs in the world.

These skills and training are used to showcase the very best of Scottish produce, with a menu heavily influenced by our natural larder.

17

G AMBA on West George Street in Glasgow's city centre is a true heavyweight on the UK cooking scene, with awards to support its reputation.

Head chef and proprietor, Derek Marshall wanted to create a restaurant that would let produce speak for itself and in 1998 that was realised with the creation of one of Glasgow's most formidable names.

The whole ethos of Gamba is simple cooking of fantastic produce, and that ethos remains the same today. Elegant surroundings complement the sophisticated, classic style of cooking, with modern touches making sure the restaurant and menu is as prominent and relevant now as it was when it first opened.

The restaurant is renowned for its fish soup and the Foodies' Guide is delighted to be able to share the secret of this famous Gamba dish.

This is a fish restaurant at the top end of the scale with a chef at the top of his game at the helm.

Gamba is one of Glasgow's most established restaurants. Situated in the city centre, space at a table in the restaurant is at a premium - but once you've secured your seat, you won't want to give it up. Head chef, Derek Marshall tells us of the importance of sustainability in driving Glasgow's food scene forward.

HE said: "Sustainability is one of the biggest points to consider for the food scene in Glasgow. Because we're a fish restaurant it's mostly about using predominantly Scottish seafood, but it's been made hard by European legislation and quotas on fishing.

"We are sustainable and that is important to our customers, but there is a responsibility on the customers as well. They have to support the independent ventures making the effort to be sustainable and local in what they buy and use.

"We're one of only a few Glasgow restaurants in the Sustainable Restaurant Association – Glasgow needs to up its game a bit with a lot of the restaurants, because that will affect everyone in the future.

"I chose the Fish Soup recipe because it is our signature dish in many ways and a best seller. Some people come to the restaurant just for the fish soup. It's a simple dish and I like simplicity. I don't like food with too many flavours, and that's what Gamba does."

GAMBA   Fish Soup

225a West George St
Glasgow G2 2ND
T: 0141 572 0899

- 27g White fish meat (haddock, cod, or whiting)
- 4 Garlic cloves
- 50g Root Ginger
- 2 Medium onions, chopped
- 50g Unsalted butter
- 3 tbsp Plain flour

- 1.15ltr Fish stock
- 1 Packet of coriander
- 50g Grated stem ginger
- 3 tbsp Tomato puree
- 450g White crab meat
- 75ml Brandy

Melt the butter over a low heat in a thick bottomed pan.
Chop the onions, garlic and root ginger and sweat in a covered pan with the butter - add brandy and reduce.
Mix in the flour and cook for five minutes on a low heat. Add the tomato puree and keep mixing. Start adding fish stock little by little, mixing all the time.
Add the white fish meat and cook for 30-40mins.
Liquidise the soup and pass through a sieve into a clean pot or bowl.
Add the crabmeat, grated stem ginger and chopped coriander.
Serve in warm soup bowls with garlic bread.

A unique selling point for the Meat Bar is their meat cocktails. This sees the guys bring 'fat washing,' which started in Manhattan, to little ol' Scotland. This involves infusing alcohol with food stuff – not just for meat. It's not scientific, just good mixology. Here is one of their favourite cocktail recipes:

Suckling Sour: 50ml Bacon infused Bourbon, 25ml Lemon Juice, 10ml Maple Syrup, 1 egg white, 20ml pressed apple juice

Method: Place all ingredients in shaker, Dry Shake (without ice), then shake with ice. Serve straight up in a Cancun style glass, garnished with a slice of crispy bacon and an apple fan.

The Meat Bar on West Regent Street in the city centre, exploded onto Glasgow's food scene after much online hype. It was a perfect example of how to utilise social media and the power of food bloggers to create a buzz, with so many people talking about the venture before the doors were even open. It hasn't disappointed.

CALVIN Stewart, head chef at the Meat Bar, told us the virtues of having a strong online presence and his thoughts on the food scene in Glasgow, as well as why he chose the dish the Meat Bar submitted: "It's definitely exciting times and part of that is from the fact a lot of people are developing a real passion for food.

"We owe some of the initial interest to social media and want to keep our online presence up. We're such a 'Facebook culture' these days, you need to be involved to get your foot in the door. So we started with a few hints and teasers online, like "Meat, coming soon" and that seemed to link in well with a lot of trends.

"A lot of people will see something mentioned as cool online, or by someone who knows what's cool, or they'll see their mates talking about going to the Meat Bar for dinner and they'll decide to go as well. It's crucial to keep that presence. But you'd like to think people don't need to sit at their computer to realise they can just come here, into the real world, and eat good food.

"Pig cheeks give a burst of flavour and we love using it as a cut and they're the centre piece of the dish, but the other flavours work really well with it without taking over. It showcases the best of ingredients and our cooking ethos for much of our menu, 'low and slow cooking'."

Crispy pigs' cheeks & piccalilli style veg

142 West Regent Street
Glasgow G2 2RQ
T: 0141 204 3605

Pigs cheeks
- 500g Iberico Pigs Cheeks
- 3 Sprigs Thyme
- 2 Garlic cloves thinly sliced
- 200ml Red cooking wine
- 300ml Beef stock
- 1 De-seeded red chilli
- 10g Roughly chopped parsley
- 2 Egg yolks
- Zest of one lemon
- 3 Bayleaf
- 100g Bread crumbs
- 2g Maldon Sea salt

Piccalilli vegetables
- 200g Small florets cauliflour
- 200g Small florets broccoli
- 200g Green beans top and tailed
- 1 Large courgette roughly chopped
- 300ml White wine vinegar
- 1 Large tbsp mustard powder
- 150g Caster sugar
- 3g Salt

Sit pigs cheeks in a roasting tray and season with the maldon salt and a pinch of black pepper. Strip thyme leaves, add to the roasting tray along with garlic, bay leaf, red wine, beef stock and half of a red chilli. Cover tray with foil and place in the oven at around 160ºC for two and a half hours or until the pigs cheeks become deliciously tender.

For the piccalilli, in a pot, bring two litres of water to the boil, adding the white wine vinegar, mustard powder and generous amount of salt and one bay leaf. Roughly cut veg to the same size and blanche in the water for two minutes. Take veg out and cool in iced water to retain its crunch. Reduce veg stock – to concentrate to a pickle, add the caster sugar. When ready, pour over drained veg till covered – place in a container with a lid and set aside in fridge. Remove cheeks from tray, keeping stock aside.

Flake cheeks into pieces in a bowl, adding the breadcrumbs, the remainder of the red chilli finely chopped, parsley, lemon zest and mix well with the egg yolk. Shape pigs cheek mix into cakes, around 80 - 90g portions and set aside in the fridge until firm enough to fry.

To build the dish, assemble some of the veg on a plate and drizzle with a little amount of the pickle stock. Lightly dust pigs cheeks in plain flour, then fry in a medium to hot pan until golden brown. Gently turn them over and continue frying until hot in the middle. To maintain amazing moistness in the middle, de-glaze the pan with a little of the cooking liquid from the tray before serving with a little sea salt on top of the crispy pigs cheeks. Rest the cheeks next to the vegetables and finish with a little Spanish olive oil.

A relative new boy to the Glasgow food scene, the Meat Bar has taken no time in making its mark on food lovers throughout the city and beyond.

Clever use of social media in the run up to its opening kept Foodies' and socialites on tenterhooks, before its sleek surroundings and carnivorous menu were made public.

Beautifully laid out, the wooden clad restaurant is incredibly comfortable, with welcoming leather seated booths and low lighting. But it is the unique menu that customers love most.

Meat, as you would expect, runs throughout - even the cocktails are meat based, using New York born 'fatwashing' to create some fantastic tipples. That continues onto the main event, with a menu offering some of the best, most unique dishes around.

The American influences can't be overlooked, from the style of cooking and the flavours involved, to the beers, such as Sam Adams, on tap to wash them down.

But for all the Americana on show, there is an underlying current of Scottish quality that makes the Meat Bar the success it is.

The finest Scottish beef and pork sits on the menu, with renowned Scottish craft beers from the likes of the Williams Brothers on hand to wash down the fine fayre.

ONE of Glasgow's oldest and most renowned venues, Rogano, is a firm favourite with celebrities visiting this magnificent city.

A regular haunt for Scotland's number one adopted crooner, Rod Stewart, Rogano sits slap bang in the city centre, and is ideally situated for paparazzi to catch a glimpse of the rich and famous.

As well as A-list clientèle, the restaurant can boast A-list décor and architecture, with the art deco design an homage to past great liners built on the Clyde.

Opened in 1935, as the Queen Mary was taking shape at the city's shipyards, the restaurant also has a reputation for A-list food, and is widely renowned as one of the best fish and seafood restaurants around.

But meat lovers and vegetarians are well catered for here too, with a variety of well thought out, excellently cooked options.

The best of Scotland's larder is on show, with fine fish and shellfish taking pride of place, and venison, lamb, and Scotch beef providing a supporting act suitable to headline any A-list show.

A well stocked bar and charming, attentive staff, further add to the restaurants virtues. Rogano's reputation precedes it and rightly so.

Andy Cumming is the head chef at one of Glasgow's busiest and most famous restaurants, Rogano.

I think Glasgow is brilliant. It's moving so far away from the quest for a Michelin Star and that's great. I'll never get a Michelin Star because I'm a big brasserie - we offer a great experience, that's what we do. The half mile stretch of Argyle Street in Finnieston at the moment is a fantastic place and there are very talented chefs there doing a great job – and they're really cool places to eat and drink as well.

"People come to Glasgow for a different experience. They come for a breath of fresh air and for the culture. Edinburgh is more the Tartan Tourist experience. The food here is more honest and we're going in the right direction now, using local, sustainable and ethical produce. We're thinking local and looking at a local audience, and at introducing cheaper cuts to that audience.

"There's always that nice thing of going into Rogano and seeing the celebrities – whether they're holding up the bar or sitting at their favourite table. I always say the golden era for us is now – it was the golden era ten years ago and will be the golden era ten years down the line. I often think I am a curator of a museum and for me it's about keeping that golden era.

"There are beautiful scenarios going on behind the scene to keep this place at the top of its game. It's about knowing your customer and knowing the Glasgow customer. They are a difficult customer to read."

Smoked Haddock Risotto and Poached Egg

11 Exchange Place
Glasgow G1 3AN
T: 0141 248 4055

Risotto
• 75g Butter
• 400g Risotto rice
• 1 Shallot (finely chopped)
• Hot fish stock
• 100g Fresh garden peas

Smoked Haddock
• 4 Fillets of undyed smoked

haddock (diced into 1 cm cubes)
• 1 Lemon
• 10g Chopped parsley
• 50g Parmesan cheese

Poached Egg
• Vinegar
• 4 Eggs

Risotto
Melt the butter in a pan.
On a high heat sweat the rice and shallots for 3-4mins.
Add hot stock gradually until it is all used up. This should take
12-15mins, until rice is almost cooked to al dente.
Add the smoked haddock and peas and cook for a further three minutes.
Finish by adding the lemon juice, parsley and Parmesan cheese.

Poached Egg
Bring a pot of water to the boil. Add a teaspoon of vinegar.
On a gentle heat swirl the water round in the pot with a wooden spoon
or whisk. Add egg into the middle of pot where the water is spinning,
which will keep it together in a neat shape. Cook until set (about three
minutes). Remove and serve.

The Butchershop Bar and Grill is one of Glasgow's trendiest and most popular restaurants. Offering 'awesome' steaks, fine wines, great cocktails and superb service, much of the restaurant's success is down to the charisma and work ethic of proprietor, James Rusk. Also the vice chairman of the Glasgow Restaurant Association, he tells us his vision for Glasgow.

THE changes in the food scene really comes down to people being able to travel and try new things more easily. We are exposed to different cultures much more now.

"Our environment has come from a sense of adventure. What Glasgow is all about as a city, is about making those things come together. It's always been a place of industry, but I don't know if the culture that was historically prevalent came through until recently. Now, more than ever, those cultures are a part of what we're doing and their influences on food is allowing us to give our food a context.

"We're not as industrial now. People take a lot more pride in food than they used to and it's more of a viable career path now than it ever was, as it is in other places in the world. This is an awesome city and country, and people are realising it now.

"We can be better, of course we can. Are we going to get it right all the time? I wish we could, but that's not the way of things, it's human nature and mistakes happen. But we are definitely going in the right direction in Glasgow and will never stop doing so.

"The street food scene is awesome. Everyone has their own areas and if everyone is innovating in the different areas, then it adds to the sum of all parts. There's something different for everyone and it's about giving a greater choice. It's about quality, not about discount culture anymore.

"Michelin Star is another aspect of dining - it's back to the sum of all parts thing. I don't think we need it, but it has it's part to play. But if you have good food, good service, and the right ambience for the experience you're trying to achieve, then that is all you need.

"There are great opportunities in Glasgow and there is so much going on. We need to be able to show that Glasgow is great and we all need to be on the same page for that.

"We're a big city and we all need to come together and become a value destination with great shopping, great tourist attractions, free museums, and a great dining scene. Everyone is doing their own thing which is great, but we all need to be ambassadors for Glasgow. We want people to want to come here for holidays and city breaks. That's what is being worked on behind the scenes. It's up to us to be pulling our weight on the ground, to make sure there is a consistent value and level of service across the board."

DRY AGEING & AWESOME STEAK

AT The Butchershop Bar & Grill the quality of our beef is our first priority. We work hand and hand with our butchers and only use the very best Scottish grass fed cattle. All our beef is hung on the bone and dry-aged to the perfect maturity for serving, ensuring a consistently high-end product every time our customers dine with us.

Beef is our business at The Butchershop Bar & Grill and a question we are often asked by our customers is 'How do you choose a quality cut of beef to cook at home?'. Here are our recommendations for choosing your steak and also some insight into the creation of awesome beef.

How to spot quality: Where is the beef you're buying from? Using an accredited Scotch supplier of beef, means that you're choosing a quality cut from Scottish cattle. We have travelled all over the world and in our opinion you can't beat Scottish beef for a truly ultimate taste sensation. Look for the Scotch beef logo on packaging and have a chat with your local butcher for more information on the beef's provenance.

Dry-ageing: The ageing process of steak is key. Hanging on the bone really develops the flavour and tenderises the meat. Don't be afraid to ask your butcher how long the beef has been hung for. At The Butchershop we hang our beef for no less than 21 days with some of our reserve cuts being hung for 50 days.

Dry-ageing causes moisture to escape from the beef and break down the tissue in the muscle creating truly tender cuts, with typically up to a third or more of weight lost during the ageing process. Bone in cuts can withstand a longer ageing process due to the relationship between bone and meat meaning that nutrients and moisture are constantly fed to the meat through the ageing process. This allows our reserve cuts at The Butchershop Bar & Grill to be aged for longer periods adding incredible depths of flavour and exceptional texture.

Marbling is a reliable indicator of quality and varies through the different types of cuts available. Look for little streaks of fat running through the meat. These little streaks melt as you cook and will penetrate the meat to give your steak even more flavour every time.

If you like heavy marbling and good fat get your local butcher to cut you a rib eye on the bone for the fullest flavour. We recommend you cook it medium to really cook out the fat and achieve that full flavour awesomeness.

Preparation, Seasoning, and Cooking: We know you may not have an industrial grill in the corner of your kitchen so here are a few tips to get the best out of your steak when cooking at home in a good, old-fashioned frying pan. If you have chosen awesome beef then you're almost there.

Butchershop Tip: Leave your steak to rest bringing it to room temperature and season with rock salt at least 20 minutes before cooking. The salted crust will help to draw the flavour out and build up a crisp, savoury layer on the outside of the meat.

GET COOKING

1055 Sauchiehall Street
Glasgow G3 7UD
T: 0141 339 2999

1. Oil the pan with a neutral oil and wait until the pan is smoking hot.
2. Lightly place the steak in the pan and begin to fry. If the pan has raised ridges, you can set your steak in at an angle in order to give it a crosshatch pattern.
3. Don't turn the steak until good seared or charred markings are achieved, then turn over and cook on the other side.
4. Cook your steak for anywhere from 3-6mins per side, depending on thickness and desired steak temp. A thicker cut will obviously require longer cooking, while a thinner cut will cook quicker. If your cut is on the bone be aware the bone draws the heat away from the meat and will be pinker at the bone than at the outer edges of the meat.
5. Once you are close to your desired steak temperature take your steak off the pan and let your steak rest for five minutes covered in foil before serving. If you don't let your steak rest properly, all the juices will spill out when you cut into it. That's because the muscle fibres tighten up during cooking, sending the juices to the centre of the cut, where the meat is still relatively rare and light. Resting the meat allows the muscle fibres to relax, sending the juices back through the entire piece of meat. Then, when you cut it up your steak, it's tender, juicy and AWESOME!

A great steak is truly a magnificent thing. Take your time, buy local, talk to your butcher and enjoy.

When speaking to chefs and food ambassadors for this project, there was one restaurant that repeatedly crept into conversation - Cail Bruich. Situated across from the Botanical Gardens on Great Western Road, the traditional Scottish restaurant is the brainchild of brothers Chris and Paul Charalambous.

HEAD chef Chris shares his thoughts on how the food scene has changed in Glasgow in recent times: "The food scene has changed dramatically. There was this pre-conception it was all deep fried food and haggis – that was our staple apparently. But that has completely changed. There are a lot of really good, well trained chefs out there who have been trained at some of the best restaurants in the world - and it shows.

"People are much more aware about food now too, especially from the customer's point of view. TV programmes have made people much more conscious about it, which has resulted in an increase in standards.

"The produce available to us in Scotland is the best in the world and we export a lot of our food to the continent for that very reason. The shellfish available to us is amazing and fishing is a major part of our economy. We have great beef, lamb and pork, and of course the best game - it's only available for six months of the year as well, so you really have to try and make the most of it when it's available to you.

"There are so many offerings out there now. If it's street food you're after, there's street food to be had, if it's Asian food, you can get a variety of that, if it's a good burger, then there are plenty of high quality burger joints to go to. Glasgow used to be overloaded with Italian restaurants, but there is so much more and there is a great variety."

725 Great Western Road
Glasgow G12 8QX
T: 0141 334 6265

Roast partridge breast, organic spelt grain, ceps and truffle sauce

For the partridge:
- 1 Whole oven ready partridge-legs and wish bone removed
- 50g Butter
- 1 Sprig thyme
- 1 Clove garlic lightly crushed

For the risotto:
- 100g Spelt
- 1 Shallot, diced
- 2 Garlic clove, slightly crushed
- 1 Sprig thyme
- 1 Bay leaf
- 100ml White wine
- 500ml Beef or chicken stock
- 50g Butter
- 50g Parmesan
- 1 tbsp Chopped chives
- 1 tbsp Chopped parsley
- 1 tbsp White truffle oil

For the mushrooms:
- 2 Medium sized ceps
- 20g Butter
- Salt and pepper
- 1tsp Chives

For the truffle sauce:
- 2 Partridge legs and carcass
- 1 Shallot-roughly chopped
- ½ Carrot-roughly chopped
- ½ Leek-white only-roughly chopped
- A small handful button mushrooms
- 100ml Red wine
- 100ml Port
- 100ml Madeira
- 500ml Veal or beef stock
- 1 Sprig thyme, 1 bay leaf, and 10 white peppercorns
- 20ml White truffle oil
- 10g Fresh black truffle, grated

Risotto:
Sweat shallot in a tablespoon of oil until translucent. Add salt, thyme, garlic, bay and sweat without colour for two more minutes – add spelt, season again and stir to coat grains. De-glaze with white wine, reduce until evaporated. Ladle in hot beef or chicken stock gradually till rice is cooked. Finish with butter, cheese, and herbs before beating vigorously till emulsified. Cover and keep warm. The risotto should be slightly wet and not stodgy.

Sauce:
Roast partridge legs and carcass in moderate oven until coloured, then set aside. Sweat shallot, carrot, leek and mushrooms in a tablespoon of oil until lightly coloured. Add herbs, garlic, peppercorns, and salt, cooking for a further two minutes. De-glaze with red wine, port and madeira, reducing by half. Add veal stock and reduce till sauce coats the back of a spoon. Cover with cling film, letting it infuse for 30mins. Strain through a fine sieve into a clean saucepan, mixing in truffle oil and grated fresh truffle. Keep warm.

Ceps:
Slice then sauté ceps in tablespoon of oil over medium heat. Add butter and salt, cooking for a further two minutes. Add two tablespoons of water to create an emulsion and reduce till mushrooms nicely glazed. Season, add herbs and drain on kitchen paper. Set aside and keep warm.

Partridge:
Heat two tablespoons of oil over a medium heat. Season partridge inside and out, then place breast side down in a pan. Cook until bird is evenly coloured, add butter and baste in the foaming butter. Add thyme, basting, then cook in moderate oven for 4-5mins till pink. Remove bird and rest for 5-10mins. Remove breasts from bird and drain on kitchen paper. Keep warm.

To assemble:
Reheat risotto in a pan and place in centre of serving bowls. Warm partridge and mushrooms, then place on top of risotto. Finally, spoon sauce over ensuring truffle is evenly distributed. Serve immediately.

31

A Manhattan styled steakhouse and cocktail bar, the Butchershop's first class reputation is primed on good quality beef and an array of expertly mixed drinks.

If the name doesn't give it away, then the menu will. This is a meat-lovers dream. From the braised beef short rib cake, to the butcher's continental charcuterie, through the d-rump classic cut steak, to the chateaubriand for two.

Priding itself on quality 100 per cent Scottish beef aged on the bone, the Butchershop serves up classic and exclusive cuts from grass fed Black Angus and Limousin cattle, supplied from breeders in Inverurie, the Borders, and Ayrshire.

But, they also provide alternative options to beef, with regular pork, chicken, fish and vegetarian dishes taking pride of place on the menu. With a changing seasonal menu, they also provide hearty salads and the freshest of produce.

The staff throughout are friendly and knowledgeable, and as diners step into the homely surroundings, they're made to feel instantly welcome and at home.

Dishes are presented by knowledgeable staff, happy to suggest appropriate wines to accompany dishes – whether by the bottle for the night, or by the glass per course.

The Butchershop is a modern day Glasgow institution.

O NE of the most talked about restaurants in Glasgow, Cail Bruich is an exciting adventure of Scottish produce brought to life with mouthwatering innovation.

Situated across from the Botanical Gardens on Great Western Road, the traditional Scottish restaurant permits the food to do most of the talking. Thankfully for the diner, it doesn't so much talk, as scream from the rooftops.

Beautiful dishes, both in sight and in taste, are delivered at the hands of head chef Chris Charalambous whose invention and finesse is supported by truly stunning techniques, resulting in some of the best food in Glasgow.

Would-be diners can choose from the market menu, showcasing fine game, poultry and seafood mains, with delicate starters and hearty desserts.

Diners can also choose from the a la carte menu or tasting menu, which allows them to experience the best of what the kitchen staff have to offer.

Nice touches in the service make the experience all the better, with dietary requirements and food allergies determined when booking by the charming and polite staff who definitely know their stuff.

Cail Bruich even have Mark Williams from Galloway Wild Foods foraging for them for some of the best herbs, ceps, and wildlife treats Scotland has to offer.

Cheese. A weakness for so many and something Scotland can boast great examples of. Whether it's world class Arran Blue, Criffel, or Dunlop Cheddar, we have some of the best around. George Mewes on Glasgow's Byres Road stocks the finest Scotland has to offer, as well as a balanced selection of world class British and Continental Artisan cheeses, and even some unusual cheeses you'd struggle to find on most supermarket shelves.

Graham Suttle, managing director of Kained Holdings, who own a host of successful restaurants, tells us about the buzz surrounding Glasgow's restaurant scene and the produce available from all over the west coast, including Ayrshire's shellfish.

SPEAKING in relation to his Finnieston restaurant, he said: "Glasgow is in an amazing place for food at the moment. I'm astounded by the true creativity - there are so many young people and newcomers to the scene as well.

"We hit a brick wall at the tail end of the 90s and start of the naughties, where big companies had taken over and it was very generic. For a point of difference in dining experience or quality, you really had to spend big. At the restaurant we use only sustainably sourced, local produce - people are concerned about where their food is coming from, so we have to be conscious about that.

"Glasgow is always going to be Edinburgh's poor cousin, both financially and socially, but there will be a massive influx of people to Glasgow in the

next few years. The city offers great value for money and just as high a quality of food. There's a real sense of community in the Glasgow food scene and that's why I came here; that's why I set up a business here and started a family here.

"We have a close relationship with McCallum's of Troon and when I was in Spain recently I saw langoustines caught by McCallum's on sale there – it just shows you how good Scotland's produce is. And that goes for our beef as well, which is some of the best in the world. Now customers are proud of their natural larder and they are thinking about what they are eating and taking more care about what they eat when out or at home. They eat at better restaurants and they think about the ingredients."

Troon Lobster, pan fried hand dived scallops

1125 Argyle Street
Glasgow
T: 0141 222 2884

For the lobster
• 2 x 600g Lobsters
For the scallops
• 6 Hand dived scallops
For the mango purée
• 3 Ripe mangos
• 50g Sugar
• 20ml Water

For the lime oil
• 50ml Lime juice
• 200ml Olive oil
For the lime sherbet
• 5 Limes
• 30g Sugar
• 20g Malic acid

To begin, boil the lobster for 15mins then cool in iced water – before serving, crack the shell and remove the meat from body part of lobster Don't discard the meat from the claw, but don't use for this dish.
For the mango purée, peel and de-seed the mango, add to the blender with the sugar and water – blend until a fine purée.
For the lime oil, whisk the lime juice and oil together. For the sherbet, zest the limes and place in a low heated oven. Add the sugar and malic acid, mixing well.
Open the scallops, remove the roe and place on a jay cloth. Pat dry and fry for two minutes on each side, or until a light golden brown.
Serve with pea shoots and slices fresh radish.

FINNIESTON is thee place to be in Glasgow, and seafood and gin specialist, the Finnieston Restaurant is the reigning jewel in the crown. Walking in from the inevitable cold, the warmth from the coal fire, mood-lighting, wooden floors and thriving atmosphere are a fine welcome for any would-be diner.

The emphasis is on freshly sourced Scottish seafood, complemented by a collection of bespoke draught beers, fine Champagnes, with seasonal menus changing as fish stocks and produce do. The cocktail menus are also changing, showcasing carefully sourced spirits from across the globe.

As well as mainstay dishes on the menu, diners have the choice of three catch of the day fish, available poached, grilled, pan-fried, or as good old fish n' chips. This is an impressive modern take on the classic, with triple-fried chips as good as they get, a pea compote packing a heap of flavour, homemade tartare sauce, and pickles, all beautifully presented in individual containers.

The menu is more expansive though, with meat and vegetarian options, a selection of starters and sides, an always impressive surf and turf option, and fine desserts.

"The Finnieston is a hidden gem," the owners boast. And rightly so.

THE Gannet has thrown its hat in the ring as contender for Glasgow's shining light continuing to excite diners since opening in 2013.

Barely standing when they took charge, the Argyle Street restaurant is now the proud home to chefs-come-businessmen, Peter McKenna and Ivan Stein. It's a far cry from the derelict ruin they bought, with the classy looking bar and 60 cover restaurant bearing testament to the duo's perseverance.

Indeed, first service at the eatery saw the culmination of over three years of work for the duo, who met whilst working at another Glasgow restaurant, where they discovered a mutual love of food, the dining experience, and going out.

As for the food, well it's as you'd expect from two professionals who have trained alongside some of the world's most impressive Michelin Star chefs. This is high-end dining in warm, relaxed, comfortable surroundings.

Their 'pre-Hydro' menu offers well priced two and three course options, where the stunning food confirms quality need not be sacrificed for value for money.

The surroundings are supported by fantastic food, great wines, beautiful beer and knowledgeable, charming staff who have a passion for what's on offer.

The Gannet is what modern dining should be about and it's a fine addition to Glasgow's restaurant scene.

Heralded as the restaurant to lead the way for Glasgow's food scene, the hype surrounding the opening of The Gannet was palpable - the end product from Peter McKenna and Ivan Stein hasn't disappointed. They talk to us about Glasgow's food scene and the pressures surrounding success.

Peter:

YOU have to treat the ingredients with care and respect - once you've got those basics down I think you're heading in the right direction. The food scene here is a lot better than what it was five years ago. The blogger scene has put a spotlight on restaurants and eating out. We have got to raise our game – you can't get away with serving the same old shite. It's about keeping things fresh and offering something new as best you can for your repeat customers.

"One of the big changes is the free marketing available to independent operators with social media. If you haven't got involved in that, I'd say your crazy.

"I'm not going to say we don't want it, but it's too presumptuous to say we will lead the way for Glasgow getting a Michelin Star. It's definitely not our focus. We're about good, casual food trying to get consistency and get a broad support from our customers. We're our own worst critics and no one will criticise what we do more than ourselves. It's very nice that people think so positively of us, but we need to be focusing on the negatives to make sure we are still improving."

Ivan:

IT takes a lot to change a food culture. Glasgow is heavily associated with fish and chips, and curry, which is fine, but you can't reinvent a food culture over night.

"There's good sustainable, fresh fish available here and we want to embrace that as well as the farmed stuff. As a country we have to meet demand and it's only going to increase with the trade deal with China, so there is a place for farmed fish, but we have to make sure the quality doesn't suffer as a result of demand.

"You like to see a lot of independent restaurants operating as that's the way forward and it's how to get the best from the market. I think the amount of chains that have come into the market in the last 10-15 years has been incredibly bad for the industry. If we have a good, thriving independent sector, then there's a lot that can be done to support that.

"Social media actually reinforces the social element to going out, to eating out, and people want to buy into being a part of something, to an experience and to a night out with others. Social media is where it's at and we have to be in amongst it."

1155 Argyle Street
Finnieston
Glasgow G3 8TB
T: 0141 2042081

Boarders Lamb rump, Parsley potatoes, Jerusalem artichoke and Olive sauce

Lamb rump: *Ask butcher to trim rump, leaving good covering of fat on top (150g portions are suffice). Brine lamb in 1kg water, 80g salt, 5g whole white pepper corns for three hours, rinse and pat dry.*

Jerusalem artichokes:
• 300g Jerusalem artichokes
• 1 Shallot
• 1 Clove garlic
• 1 Good sprig of thyme
• 50g Cream
• 100g Chicken stock

• Seasoning. rock salt for cooking on x 100g
• 50g Butter

Parsley potatoes:
• 500g Maris piper
• 100g Rock salt for cooking on
• 20ml Milk
• 50ml Cream
• 100g Butter
• 2 Cloves garlic
• 1 Bunch of parsley
• Seasoning

Olive sauce:
• 1kg Lamb bones
• 750ml Chicken stock
• 250ml Quality veal stock
• 100g Shallots
• 2 Cloves garlic
• 200g Tomatoes
• 20g Tomato purée
• 1 Good sprig of Rosemary
• 50g Black olives in brine
• 2g Cumin
• 5g White pepper corns

Jerusalem artichokes - roast on top of the rock salt for 45mins or until tender. Scoop out pulp, reserving for purée. Dehydrate skins in a very low oven – can take up to six hours.

Sweat shallots and garlic in butter, once soft add cooked artichoke, chicken stock and thyme. Cook till stock reduced then add cream. Bring to boil, season, strain of excess liquid, and purée– season to taste.

Parsley potatoes – bake potatoes on rock salt at 180°C until tender. Scoop out and pass through a sieve, keep warm by covering. Infuse cream/milk with garlic and seasoning. Mix cooked potato with liquids, then beat in butter. Blanch parsley in boiling water, 'shock' in ice water and blend to a bright green purée.

Olive sauce – roast lamb bones for 45mins at 180°C

till golden brown. Sweat shallots and garlic till soft. Add tomatoes, tomato purée and rosemary; cook till most of water has evaporated and mix is compote like. Add bones, stocks and spices, bring to boil, then simmer for 45mins. Pass through sieve and reduce until sauce consistency. Roughly chop pitted olives, add to finished sauce.

To serve:
Roast the lamb until centre of meat reaches 57°C
Deep fry artichoke skins till crisp, filling with the heated purée.
Heat potato purée with enough of the parsley purée as required to reach vivid green colour – add fresh parsley for flavour.
Finish the dish with a good amount of the olive sauce.

39

Writer, comedian, Celebrity Masterchef finalist, and food ambassador, Hardeep Singh Kohli shares his love of food with us, along with his thoughts on Glasgow's food scene - he also tells us what TV show Masterchef meant to him.

HE said: "Food is so intimate and epic, it's so powerful. I can smell my mum's cooking now and be transported to being four years old again, sitting in the kitchen – there's nothing else that can do that.

"Glasgow is still great curry-wise, pound for pound it's probably my favourite city to have curry. It's still authentically Punjabi influences here. In London there are thousands more Indian restaurants of course, but they are Bangladeshi, so you are three steps removed – Bangladeshi chefs cooking Punjabi food is the norm there, whereas Glasgow you still have authentic Punjabi.

"And I don't know another city where people can go into an Indian restaurant and know the names of those serving them and their wife's name, or where they went on holiday. That's totally unique to Glasgow.

"But we're a city of extremes and it's difficult to tell if we're heading in the right direction, because we are still in recession. I think the food scene has lost its way a little. What I find bizarre is that Glaswegians have money to spend on fashion and other things, but not on food.

"Street food is a great way forward and that is where genuine change will arise in terms of food culture – I'm astonished there isn't more of a West Indian food scene taking off, but I'm excited to try the Fire in Babylon street food stuff. Caribbean and North Indian food are very similar in terms of spices, so I think it could be successful here.

"There are definitely some gems though. I used to live in Wee Saigon in London and having eaten at the Hanoi Bike Shop just off Byres Road, I can tell you, it can hold its head high with the best of Vietnamese restaurants.

"What feels positive to me is that, in a time of recession, I would have expected chains to come in and take over, but that hasn't happened. Passionate individuals, who believe in food and the importance of it, are the ones committing to the future.

"Masterchef changed my life, it gave me credibility in the food world at the very top levels. I'm friends with Michelin Star chefs and I can cook in La Gavroche anytime I want – that's what Masterchef has allowed me to do. I would love to be the curator of food in a way or open a 40 cover restaurant and cook the food I want to cook. If people like it, great – if not, then it doesn't matter.

"Food is so democratising – we're Scottish and we love food and it doesn't matter who you are. You can have two massively heterosexual men standing in a Michelin Star kitchen feeding each other little spoonfuls of food, a wee bit of seared foie gras on toasted brioche, and no one would think anything of it. It's part of who we are as a nation now."

Hardeep's 'Aloo Tikki'

Boil half a dozen medium sized potatoes, skin on, in salty water. Whilst they cook, combine your spices – so, a teaspoon of coriander powder, a teaspoon of garam masala, a teaspoon of salt and the same of black pepper.

Add to that the zest of a lime and lemon, and the juice of the lemon and the juice from half of the lime. Finely chop a handful of coriander stalks and a few green chillies adding to the mixture.

Once the tatties have cooked, immediately mash, or better still, rice them. Add the spice mix and give it a good big stir. Let the mixture cool in the fridge before you shape the spiced mash into burger sized patties. Fry in some butter and rapeseed oil, browning on both sides. Serve with tamarind chutney.

THIS is a great dish widely eaten throughout Vietnam and is a staple in many Vietnamese homes that can be made with just about any type of fish. Although traditionally cooked in a brown clay pot, you can use any heavy bottomed sauce pan. It has been a regular feature in the Hanoi Bike Shop and is loved by customers and staff alike.

Emily MacKay, manager at Glasgow's first Vietnamese restaurant, the Hanoi Bike Shop, "The Glasgow food scene is in a great place at the moment. There's a noticeable 'foodie' buzz that wasn't quite as prominent 5-10 years ago, which shows in the increasing variety of cuisines available and new restaurants opening up.

"In general I think people are taking a much more relaxed approach to eating out, where the importance is more on the integrity and quality of the produce and less on the formality of the

surroundings. Of course you can still go for your high-end fine dining, but you can also enjoy the same top quality in a relaxed and very social setting, such as we have created in the Bike Shop.

"The public's interest in cooking and experimenting with food has grown more and more, and it can only be a good thing for Glasgow to have people more aware and more interested in food. Whether it's for traditional Scottish restaurant, pop-up world cuisine, or a street food market, the demand is there for good quality, no-nonsense, wholesome dining."

Ca Kho To: Ginger Caramel Fish

Ruthven Lane
Glasgow
T: 0141 334 7165

- 6 Fllets of mackerel
- Vegetable oil to fry

For caramel sauce:
- 20g Galangal peeled – fresh ginger works just as well
- 4 Garlic cloves peeled
- 1 Long red chilli
- 4 Shallots peeled and roughly sliced

- 400ml Coconut milk
- 200g Caster sugar
- 100ml Fish sauce

To garnish:
- Fresh coriander, roughly chopped
- Spring onion, sliced
- Red chilli sliced

Blitz ginger, garlic, shallots and chilli together in food processor to a smooth paste consistency.

Place a medium sized, heavy based saucepan on medium heat until hot, then add paste, turning heat to low – cook for approx 10mins, stirring occasionally.

Add sugar and cook for a further five minutes or until it starts to caramelise.

Add coconut milk and fish sauce, reducing by a quarter – set aside.

Adjust seasoning to taste using fish sauce – ultimately the caramel should be a lovely balance of sweet, salt and ginger.

Place a frying pan on a high heat and add a little oil. Once hot place fish skin side down in the pan for 3-5mins.

Add caramel sauce and simmer on a low heat until fish is cooked through. Garnish with coriander, spring onion and chilli. Serve with steamed jasmine rice

La Parmigiana is a Glasgow institution. Looking over the River Kelvin in the heart of the city's leafy West End, it's a fantastic example of Glasgow's embedded Italian culture, showcasing the best Italian dishes using Scottish produce.

OWNER and former head chef, Sandro Giovanizzi tells us his thoughts on the food scene: "The main change is that people are so much more travelled and they know what a plate of pasta should be like. They know how fish should be prepared – they now know what to expect. As a result, restaurants have improved as has the food scene. It's definitely for the better.

"Our fish is all from local producers and Scottish fish is the best there is - air dried Scottish beef is fabulous too, it melts like butter in the mouth.

"Italian tourists know us and they know where to come to eat good Italian food in Glasgow. We hope to welcome many of them over the next year."

447 Great Western Road
Glasgow G12 8HH
T: 0141 334 0686

Owner Sandro
and head chef,
Peppino

Cacciucco alla Livornese

- 4 Garlic cloves
- 2 Chillies
- 4 tbsp Chopped parsley
- 1 Stalk chopped celery
- 1 Cup olive oil
- 1 Medium chopped carrot
- 200g Peeled tomatoes
- 2 Medium chopped onion
- 12 Slices crusty bread

- 400g Mixture of Cephalopoda molluscs, such as squid, octopus cuttlefish
- 400g Mixture of shelled molluscs, such as mussels, clams, cockles
- 400g Crustaceans - mixture of Dublin Bay prawns, shrimps, crabs, lobster or whatever is available

- 300g Mixture of white fish, like gurnard, cod, coley red mullet or whatever is available
- 300g Firmer fish - mixture of dogfish, halibut, monkfish or whatever is available
- 300g Mix of fish heads to make stock
- 1 Glass red wine

Clean all the fish, with particular attention to the mussels - preserve the heads to make a stock. Cut larger fish in two or three pieces to allow a uniform cooking time. Cut the octopus and cuttlefish into strips.

To make the stock, add fish heads and any bones from filleting, together with celery, carrot and one onion finely chopped to a large pot. Add the parsley, one clove of garlic and salt and just cover with water. Bring to boil and simmer for 30-40mins.

In the meantime, heat the oil in a large saucepan and fry the finely chopped parsley, one clove of garlic, chilli and one chopped onion over medium heat. When onion has taken on a nice golden colour, add the strips of cuttlefish and octopus and season. At this point turn up the heat, as soon as the fish starts to colour add the wine and the coarsely chopped tomatoes and continue cooking for about 30mins until cuttlefish and octopus become soft and the sauce is dry. Meanwhile, the fish stock will be ready. Drain and set aside. Add the stock you have obtained to the cooking sauce and resume the cooking. At this point add the mussels, clams and cockles. When these have opened, start to add the firmer fish like the Dublin Bay Prawns, shrimps, dogfish, monkfish and halibut. Then continue with the white fish, cover and cook for about 15mins.

For the Bruschetta, toast the slices of bread, rub them with garlic, and brush with olive oil and place onto the serving dishes – simple.

Divide the cacciucco onto the bread and serve hot, accompanied by more bruschetta. Serve with a good Vermentino di Bolgheri. Buon Appetito!

Glasgow's West End is hardly short on options for eating out, but finding something unique and of real quality is more challenging.

Thank heavens then for places like the Hanoi Bike Shop, Glasgow's first Vietnamese restaurant, offering individuality and quality in spades.

A step inside the Ruthven Lane venue will transport diners to Saigon, with the aromas of traditional Vietnamese cooking filling the compact, well laid out dining area, which is decked out with wooden tables, benches and stools.

The whole atmosphere is relaxed, matched by the relaxed but well trained staff who are fully knowledgeable of the menu.

A step away from the traditional a la carte menu, diners are encouraged to share any three dishes between two, brought out dish by dish when ready, ensuring everything stays hot and fresh.

Whether it's the five-spice chilli prawns, with soy salad cream, or marinated chicken, brought to life with spicy, refreshing flavours like chilli and ginger, the dishes on offer are a delight to experience.

The Hanoi Bike Shop is a welcome shot in the arm for Glasgow, serving truly authentic Vietnamese food and a little slice of the culture – it's a must try.

Set in one of Glasgow's most vibrant areas, Ox and Finch has a kitchen team that has poled up more than its fair share of restaurants, art galleries, glitzy parties, and grand prix grids.

And with a culinary team boasting the former head chef of the McLaren Formula 1 team, a chef trained at the hands of Gordon Ramsay and Jason Atherton, and a former sous chef from the Michelin Starred Martin Wishart restaurant at Loch Lomond, you could say the Kelvingrove venue is somewhere brimming with talent and creativity.

And you'd be right. Head Chef and proprietor, Jonathan MacDonald has sculpted a team and restaurant that provides some of the finest food you'll find in Glasgow.

Having left the hoi polloi of the Formula 1 circuit and ditched the bureaucracy of the London restaurant scene, he set up his very successful SCOOP catering and brilliant Street Food Cartel ventures.

That creativity paved the way for the Ox and Finch, which serves up a fresh selection of flavours and taste experiences, with seasonal food served in a sociable sharing style, ensuring a firm focus on the best quality produce, preparation, cooking techniques and presentation.

Expect tartar of roe deer, hazelnuts and mustard; 36 month-aged Jamón Ibérico de Bellota with Catalan tomato toast; and braised ox cheek, roast cauliflower puree, thyme and bacon gremolata, for which you can find a variation recipe in the Foodies' Guide.

MUCH like the cult character it's named after, Lebowski's in Glasgow's Finnieston area is a trailblazer that redefines the pub grub concept.

And, like the Dude himself, the bar is the epitome of laid back, with a relaxed and funky atmosphere you'll never want to leave.

Ideal for small groups, there is also a designated area that can be reserved for larger parties. One of the coolest bars in Glasgow's trendy West End, it is also one of the closest to the Hydro and ideal for pre or post concert food and drink.

Lebowski's is renowned for its generous, towering burgers and you can find the recipe for the original and best in the Foodies' Guide. A menu filled with fan favourites, only the best Scottish produce is used, from meat patties to artisan breads.

The variety on offer is sure to satisfy all, whether looking for breakfast, lunch, dinner, or just bar snacks with drinks.

And hungry diners who pop in for food won't be disappointed, with a substantial menu backed up by a fine selection of bottled beers, craft beers, and cocktails.

There is also the best selection of White Russians this side of Las Vegas. A definite strike.

THERE are fewer more vibrant spots in Glasgow's West End than Kelvinbridge, which hosts one of the city's longest running and most vibrant Italian restaurants.

La Parmigiana has been proudly serving Glasgow some of the best Italian food around since 1978, with the Giovanazzi family firmly at the helm throughout that tenure.

And their hard work, passion and determination can still be seen now, with a restaurant renowned for its elegance and tradition.

The best of Scottish produce, cooked in authentic Italian ways, results in some of the finest food in the West End. And over the years it has resulted in numerous awards and widespread recognition, regularly appearing in lists of the top ten Italian eateries in the UK.

Mouthwatering dishes are complemented by the well-stocked bar and fine wine list, which serves up exclusively Italian wines and after dinner Grappa.

Friendly, knowledgeable staff are always attentive, but manage to maintain a relaxed atmosphere throughout the restaurant, which only serves to heighten the diner's enjoyment of this Glasgow Italian great.

Graham Suttle of Kained Holdings, tells us how the Lebowski burger paved the way for a different style of eating out experience in Glasgow.

HE said: "We were former doormen and bar managers, and we wanted to do more in the trade.

"We knew good and bad points from the industry and wanted to create something using just the best stuff, that was different, cool and good. Even our name is synonymous with cool and relaxed – Lebowski's.

"We wanted to get food you could shout about and that happened for us in 2006/7 with the Lebowski burger. We wanted to offer something different and that went along with the organic movement at the time, which merged into the sustainability, local food movement. We were already there and the Lebowski burger was the catalyst for bars and clubs around Scotland to ask why it was working and how could they get on board.

"Our burger patties are nothing other than ground up steak, salt and pepper, and that's all you need. We teamed up with an artisan baker and designed our own roll that we thought was ideal for what we wanted. A lot of independent operators made the decision to do similar and it has worked."

The Godfather Burger

1008 Argyle Street
Glasgow G3 8LX
T: 0141 564 7988

Burger:
• 220g Cairnhill Farm steak – a flank and rump blend
Bun:
• Artisan foccacia bun from Essads Bakery in Glasgow

Basil aioli:
• 50ml Mayonnaise
• 3 Basil leaves
• Half a clove of garlic
• 10ml Olive oil
• Seasoning
Chilli relish:
• 15g Red, green and yellow
  pepper
• 15g Red onion
• 15g Pickled gherkin
• 10g Red chilli

• 10g Light brown sugar
• 50ml Ketchup
• 10ml White wine vinegar
• Seasoning
Mozzarella fritter:
• 30g Slice of mozzarella
• One egg,
• 25ml Milk
• 30g Homemade panko
  breadcrumb
• Seasoning
Parma Ham

Half a red pepper, de-seed and place under grill until skin blackens. Place into iced water for five minutes, peel skin and reheat under grill before building the burger.

For the Parma ham crisp, cover a small baking tray in parchment carefully place one slice of Parma ham on top, rub a little olive oil onto meat with a twist of black pepper. Place an equal sized piece of parchment on top and gently press down, bake for 20mins at 180°C. Remove from oven and carefully place onto a cooling rack.

For the aioli, place all items into a food processor and blitz for 30 seconds.

For the fritter, dip mozzarella in seasoned flour then egg, before dipping in panko crumb. Deep fry at 180°C until golden.

For chilli relish, fine dice peppers, onions, gherkins and chilli. Gently fry in a little olive oil for three minutes, add brown sugar and cook until fully dissolved. Add ketchup and vinegar and reduce by one quarter.

The burger patty is cooked 2-3minutes either side, turning just once. Finish in the oven for five minutes at 180°C.

Assemble the components and serve the burger with beef tomato, sliced red onion and lollo rosso lettuce.

OX and Finch is a modern Scottish 80-cover restaurant owned by chef Jonathan MacDonald, founder of Scoop Events/Street Food Cartel and former chef with the McLaren F1 team.

He told us: "Michelin Stars have come and gone in Glasgow. That aspiration isn't there as much and a lot of the top Glasgow restaurants are institutions and have a great deal of staying power. Mother India for instance, is an iconic venue and a great example of that. But there is a great deal of quality without pretension in Glasgow, and that's true in all walks of life. Michelin has changed as well, so places like Stravaigin, La Valle Blanche, the Finnieston are getting recommendations. Customers are going to these places because they want something different.

"Quirky, cosy, different places seem to do very well in Glasgow. People's impression of the city would change if it were to chase the Michelin Star. We're in a good place and going in the right direction. Glasgow has great variety and a vibrant scene, with

a lot of different cultures – it's got more of that than anywhere else in Scotland and it does it very well. The Babu Kitchen stuff for instance, is great and for me personally the street food scene is one of the most exciting things going on just now.

"This is a great period of tourism for Scotland and it will market the country very well, especially the food scene.

"Ox and Finch will focus on really good, quality, casual dining, with some international influences and different flavours that let the good quality Scottish produce speak for itself.

"We chose the recipe because it is simple and produce led. It is something that is quite affordable and is easier to do than you might imagine. It reflects what we do as well and has an international influence."

Braised ox cheeks, celeriac, shitake mushrooms and bacon and thyme gremolata

920 Sauchiehall Street
Glasgow G3 7TF

- 3 Ox cheeks- outer sinew removed and halved into portions
- Bottle of red wine
- 2 Carrots cut as for mirepoix
- 1 Onion cut as for mirepoix
- 2 Sticks of celery cut as for mirepoix
- 2 Bulbs of garlic
- 2 Tomatoes quartered
- 8 Sprigs of thyme
- 1 tbsp Stock syrup

- 1tbsp Flour
- 2ltr Chicken stock
- 1ltr Veal stock
- 1 Large celeriac
- 500g Shitake mushrooms
- 200g Smoked pancetta diced into lardons
- 500g Butter
- 500ml Double cream
- 200g Panko breadcrumbs
- Vegetable oil

Marinade ox cheeks in the wine with a sprig of thyme and handful of mirepoix for 12 hours. Drain off ox cheeks, reserving the wine.

Sear the ox cheeks in a smoking hot pan on all sides until evenly caramelised – season liberally with fine salt. Set aside.

Turn down heat in pan, add in a half block of butter, the mirepoix and thyme – slowly caramelise veg until nicely coloured – roughly 15mins.

Once veg is coloured add in flour, cooking out for a minute or two, before returning to a high heat – add in the reserved cooking wine, reduce until a syrupy consistency. Now add in the stock syrup, cook for a minute, and add in chicken and veal stock, tomatoes and a garlic bulb halved – bring to the boil and add ox cheeks in, bringing back to the boil.

Cover with a cartouche and oven cook at approx 180°C for 2-3 hours turning occasionally.

While ox cheeks are cooking, peel celeriac and cut the centre into a large even square, then cut the square into inch dice, reserving the trim for puree.

For the puree, put the reserved celeriac trim into a pan with two litres of water and 20g of salt. Bring up to a gentle simmer and cook until soft. When soft, drain the celeriac into a colander and put back into the pan with enough double cream to nearly cover.

Put back on a very low heat until cream has reduced right down. Blitz the celeriac, pass through a chinois, season and set aside in a warm place.

For the roasted celeriac, heat a couple of tablespoons of vegetable oil in a wide bottomed stainless steel pan until smoking hot, then add celeriac (only add enough so there is plenty of room in the pan to quickly colour the dice). Season well, colour on each side quickly, then add in the butter a few knobs at a time until it starts foaming, then add a few cloves of garlic and two sprigs of thyme.

Make sure butter does not burn by adding more butter to regulate the temperature if needed. Cook until dice is cooked through with a nice golden brown colour. Strain through a colander to get rid of the excess fat.

For the roast shitake, half the mushrooms and follow the same procedure as the roast celeriac.

In a smoking hot pan add a little oil and brown off the lardons releasing the fat, and making sure they crisp up. Then add butter and wait till it foams before adding in the thyme, followed by the panko breadcrumbs. Stir frequently until breadcrumbs have soaked up the foaming butter and have turned a nice golden brown colour. Take from the pan and drain on kitchen paper to take off any excess fat.

Be careful not to season throughout the process as the bacon can sometimes be very salty. Only season at the end.

Pierce the ox cheeks with a tooth pick to check if they are ready, there should be no resistance whatsoever. If ready, leave to cool in the liquor before removing.

Strain the liquor though a conical strainer then through a chinois into a clean pan and reduce until the desired consistency is met. Put the ox cheeks back into the sauce to warm through.

To serve, put a large spoonful of celeriac puree into the centre of each warm plate, rest the ox cheek on top, scatter the roast mushrooms and celeriac over and around the ox cheek and top the ox cheek with a few tablespoons of the sauce. Then sprinkle the gremolata over the top and serve.

GROUP director, Des Mullen shared his thoughts on the food scene in Glasgow: "For a long time Glasgow has done the middle level of the market really well - the last three or four years, we have done the top level much better. It's not fine dining, or Michelin Star and I don't think that would work here. But we have really great, privately owned places doing very well.

"We are going in the right direction. We are much better than where we were, even just five years ago. Ten years ago it was all about curry and haggis. But now there is a vast diversity of foods, authentically produced by people here with an indigenous background.

"The street food scene is a very good thing. I think it would have been more successful, and successful a few years ago, if there was less red tape involved. It just hampers development. To serve food outside in Glasgow, you'd spend about a month filling in risk assessment forms. There's a demand, so that should tell the authorities something.

"I like modern British food. I went to Cail Bruich just before Christmas and had one of the best meals I've had in my life. I had duck hearts on spelt risotto to start, pork belly and duck fat potatoes for main, and a panacotta for desert. It was fantastic."

53

Shetland salmon in a lightly spiced batter with pea puree

652-654 Argyle Street
Glasgow G3 8UF
T: 0141 221 8188

Pea Puree Ingredients
• 500g Frozen peas
• 50g Finely chopped onion
• Vegetable stock cube

Batter Ingredients
• 3 Eggs

• 1 tsp Curry powder
• 1 tsp Turmeric
• Chopped soft herbs
• Salmon – 150g fillets per
  person, sliced thinly

Pea Puree:
Sweat off seasoned onions in a little oil. Add peas and stock cube, cook until peas are piping hot. Blend with a stick blender adding water till purée.

Egg Batter:
Whisk together thoroughly, do not season

Salmon:
Dust salmon with flour then dip in batter. Pan fry in hot oil, turning before a flash under the grill. Because the salmon is sliced thinly, it will cook quickly, so keep your eye on it. Place the salmon on the puree and serve.

THE Buttery is a Glasgow institution and deserves to be showcased with respect and integrity.

In taking over the beautiful, elegant premises in 2007, the Two Fat Ladies have done just that, strengthening the restaurant's mantle as one of Glasgow's finest eateries.

The venue is warm, welcoming, and incredibly charming, with a fine nod to Scottish culture and décor – broody tones, stained glass, ornaments, knick-knacks, and luxurious antique furniture set a rich tone, yet the atmosphere is captivating and relaxing.

As for the food, it is more than a match for the splendour of the surroundings. Tried and tested recipes from the Two Fat Ladies repertoire showcase the best of Scottish produce and the best of the chef's wares.

But it's more than the fish portfolio the Two Fat Ladies' are known for, with beautiful game, poultry, and beef taking pride of place on a menu that offers fantastic value for money.

A chicken risotto, with hints of citrus and cream is a fine starter, whilst Gressingham duck and poached plums is a fine follow on. But they know their seafood and they do it so very well.

The Shandon Belles in the basement of the Buttery opened in October 2008 as a bistro, offering a counter to the classic dining on the ground floor. A fine experience to be had all round.

Spaghettini with crab

64 Ingram Street
Glasgow G1 1EX
T: 0141 572 1472

- 450g Fresh crab meat (white)
- 500g Uncooked spaghettini
- 8 Dark anchovy fillets - diced
- 1 Small punnet cherry tomatoes, halved
- 1 Fresh chilli, diced

- 4 Garlic cloves, finely chopped
- ½ cup finely diced fresh parsley
- 125ml White wine
- 6 tbsp Extra virgin olive oil
- Salt and pepper

Bring a large pot of water to the boil. Place another pot or large saute pan over a medium heat, add the olive oil to the pan and heat through.

Add dry spaghettini to boiling water. Now begin making the sauce while pasta cooks for around 3-4mins or until al dente. Add chilli and garlic to heated oil and cook for one minute, making sure not to burn garlic.

Now add anchovy fillets, cooking until dissolved. Turn up the heat slightly, throwing in the halved cherry tomatoes. Continue to cook for a further two minutes. Add wine – once bubbling, add crab and heat through. Now add parsley and seasoning, mix through. Remember, anchovies add salt so be careful not to over season.

Drain pasta once cooked and add to crab mixture with a little water from pasta pot – toss pasta and sauce together, then serve.

55

REVIEW

GLASGOW has never been short of Italian influence and neither has its food scene.

One of the best on show, serving up great food in a relaxed, comfortable environment, is the Italian Kitchen.

With its roots firmly planted in the Merchant City, the restaurant opened in 2004 – thankfully, quality hasn't wavered and it's still as good as when it first opened.

A warm, friendly welcome awaits any diner, with the wood-fired pizza oven, pine flooring and varnished tables helping to serve up a small slice of Italy in the heart of Glasgow.

And that's matched by the kitchen staff, who serve up fine Italian fayre with arguably Glasgow's best pizzas a mainstay of the menu. The upmarket Italian uses only the finest ingredients, bringing dishes that extra bit of quality at no great cost to the diner.

And for those looking for something more authentic and high end, the pasta dishes and specials on offer are – well, special.

Braised rabbit ravioli with a sage reduction, the veal with Parma ham in a white wine and sage sauce, or roasted duck in a rich marsala sauce, with crisp pancetta, all showcase the quality at work in the kitchen.

As Glasgow's many Italian restaurants go, there are few quite as good as this.

REVIEW

SUCCESS in the catering business started off for Guy Cowan with his location catering business, Reel Food.

Thankfully for diners though, he decided to share his love of food and Hollywood by setting up his own restaurant, Guy's in the heart of the Merchant City.

With an eclectic menu showcasing his own, personal dining preferences, the restaurant mirrors his passion for cooking. Indeed, nowhere else in the city would you find sushi, sashimi, mince and tatties, steak tartare or a variety of homemade ravioli on the same menu.

The menu is matched by an equally eclectic décor, which showcases Guy's fun side and love of films, with A-list memorabilia adorning wood panelled walls. The cosy, romantic, perfectly lit restaurant, sets the perfect ambience for an evening with friends, or just a table for two.

Guy's uses only the finest, local ingredients sourced from independent producers, offering the ideal platform for Scottish produce.

That includes Aberdeen Angus Beef, Scotch Lamb, grass fed veal from Sunnyside Farm in Sanquhar, and shellfish from MacCallum's of Troon.

Spaghetti with Pork and Veal Ragu

24 Candleriggs
Merchant City
Glasgow G1 1TD
T: 0141 552 1114

- 250g Lean minced pork
- 250g Lean minced veal
- 2 Large onions, peeled and medium diced
- 10 Cloves garlic, finely chopped
- 1 Red chilli, optional, finely chopped
- 2 Cans chopped tomatoes, drained
- ½ Bottle dry white wine, like a Gavi or a Pinot Grigio
- ¼ Pint double cream.

- Basil leaves and stalks, separated
- Parsley, lots of it finely chopped
- Virgin olive oil
- Knob salted butter
- Salt and pepper
- Good quality spaghetti or pasta of your choice, preferably make your own
- Small piece of fresh parmesan reggiano, to grate over the finished plate

In a large pot, soften onions, garlic and chilli in olive oil whilst stirring over a medium heat until they turn opaque. Separately, brown meats in another pot before adding to onion mix. Add white wine, keep stirring and cook down until wine has all but gone. Pour in drained tomatoes and chopped basil stocks, keep stirring. Season with salt and pepper. Add cream and cook for a little longer. Finally adjust the seasoning to taste, add a couple of tablespoons of olive oil, lots of shredded basil and chopped parsley. Total cooking time around two-and-a-half hours. Meanwhile, add water to a separate pot and salt well, bringing to a rolling boil. Pop in the pasta and cook, stirring frequently, till ready. Drain and toss with olive oil and butter, add to pan with the sauce and mix well. Serve with bread and some freshly grated parmesan, enjoy. **Guy's Top Tip: don't use too much sauce, big mistake.**

WITH its distinctive art work and powerful heat, Glasgow Megadeath hot sauce burst onto our food shelves over two years ago, leading to a hot sauce craze. From online only sales for friends and families, the product can now be found on the shelves of some of the city's biggest supermarkets and independent traders. The success of the product was down to one man.

That man is The Glasgow Chilli Guy and he tells us how his venture came about and some of the best places to go for a little spice in the city.

"It started as something for friends, making up hot sauces and barbecue sauces, then it took off, with bars and restaurants across the city using it as their table sauce. The first run was of three dozen for the two styles of sauce - neither sold that well. Then in December 2012 I sold about 3000 – it was a big step up. A year later and I couldn't keep up at Christmas – I thought I was ahead of the game, but I got wiped out with demand.

"I initially bought 100 glass bottles and jars and wanted to sell them to cover my cost, then leave it. But it really took off. The Man vs. Food programme and burger bar explosion had a lot to do with it, but I didn't know there was as much of a demand or desire for hot sauce and extreme spice in Glasgow.

"Lupe Pinto's on Great Western Road said they wanted more than the sauces, so I started to try more and came up with the Hellish Relish, and Mega Hot Nuts. But some people started to complain it wasn't as hot as they wanted - it wasn't that they didn't like the product, they just wanted more heat. I made a point to contact everyone that felt like that and refunded them. That led me to come up with the Glasgow Megadeath Hardcore Mental Hot Sauce.

"The product is good quality, it's not just flavourless heat from capsicum extract - I use the best quality chillis. What I'm finding though is the Naga chillies I use are in short supply now, and because I'll only use the best, sometimes it's hard to get them when I need. The first batch of Hardcore used 500 Naga chillis for a 50 litre batch, but they sell out so fast now.

"Glasgow folk love a curry and there's a huge demand for it here - it has become part of our culture. Scotland has a great history with Jamaica and that's where the name Scotch Bonnet comes from, and heat fits in well here. Spices work well with our meats and fish, and they're a lot more prevalent now. I can use six or seven different chillis in my cooking sourced from shops and stalls in Glasgow thanks to the different cultures in the city - it's here to stay and so is our love of heat. Hot sauce will be a main condiment very soon. Don't get me wrong though, hot sauces and fine dining don't marry together that well and I don't see many Michelin Stars coming from using such heat.

"If I'm eating out I'll quite often eat spicy food – the guys at Mother India know if I'm in I'll order a South Indian Garlic Chilli Chicken and they bring me a bowl of fresh green chillis on the side because I love it. But I like variety and trying something different.

"Buddy's have hit the nail on the head with their burgers and BBQ and they have a good hot wings challenge. It's definitely doable though and it's a great place to go and enjoy the challenge for a bit of fun, as well as a great menu. For real heat, I would go there, any of the traditional Indian restaurants in the city, or the Squid and Whale."

Using the knowledge he gained whilst exploring his dual citizenship with the US, Chris May, proprietor of Buddy's BBQ and Burgers, went about setting up a successful takeaway in the Southside of Glasgow. Having been crowned Glasgow's best burger, and having attained a huge loyal following both in store and online, the hype and demand for a sit in Buddy's diner started to grow - and Chris duly obliged.

H E said: "I have probably seen more states than most Americans. I fell in love with barbecue flavours and tastes and became a barbecue hobbiest then got quite serious about it. There are two different techniques; barbecuing, which is low heat and slow cooking; then there is grilling, which is cooking over high heat quickly.

"I spent a lot of time mastering both and spent a lot of time in Reno, Northern Nevada. They have two extremes of weather, from 20 below in the winter, to 40 degrees Celsius in the summer – and I've barbecued in both.

"It's been wonderful since we started and really well received. The menu hasn't been influenced by Scotland, it's definitely an American menu, but the produce is all Scottish and we have some of the best

produce in the world. I don't think you can get better than Scottish pork, and the beef is great.

"The beef mince we use is slightly fatty and it's made really thin. The flavour comes from the crust of the burger, so if it's too thick it gets dry and it's not as flavoursome. Our burgers are 100 per cent Scottish beef and they are always cooked well done – the way they should be. There is no binders used, no egg or breadcrumbs, and minimum seasoning.

"I don't think a place like this would have been accepted in Scotland 10-15 years ago. We are moving away from the fine dining idea and more towards the street food concept in Glasgow. But we put fine dining levels of work into our very low brow product, and I think that's good. It should be about putting out really good food without any attitude."

Philly Cheese Steak

44 Skirving Street
Glasgow G41 3AJ
T: 0141 632 5417

- 12 Inch soft white sub roll
- 250g Sirloin cut in strips
- 100g White mushrooms sliced

- 75g Diced yellow onion
- 75g Diced green peppers
- 100g Emmental cheese, sliced

Heat frying pan with oil to medium heat
Add beef for 90secs
Add onion and pepper for 90secs
Lightly toast sub roll
Add mushrooms 60secs
Push pan contents together and lay cheese on top, cover and turn down
heat until melted 60secs
Add to sub roll

REVIEW

AFTER picking up some of the best barbecue and grill cooking knowledge from his time in America, Chris May set to opening up his own place here in the Southside of Glasgow.

Buddy's was born and burger enthusiasts from across Scotland were grateful to him for that, with a place now providing a proper American dining experience.

Having been crowned Glasgow's best burger in 2013 for its Western Burger from their takeaway premises on Skirving Street, Chris and his team set to establishing their new diner. That saw the opening of Buddy's Bar, Diner, Grill on Pollokshaws Road and it has been a success since doing so.

Burgers, pulled pork sandwiches, barbecue ribs, and hot wings, are supported by other American favourites such as mac n' cheese, barbecue beans, and fantastic coleslaw. And even better for lovers of spice, the hot wings are made up using the Glasgow Mega Death Hot Sauce.

This is proper American cooking at its best and it's right on your doorstep. The surroundings are comfortable and welcoming, with a tip of the cap to American culture.

Former head chef of the Ubiquitous Chip, Ian Brown started his own restaurant in the affluent area of Giffnock in Glasgow's Southside in 2010. It has been a success, despite the crunch of the recession, testimony to the reputation the East Kilbride native has built for himself.

IAN told us: "The food scene here is getting a lot better. The lettuce, cucumber, tomato garnish has disappeared from everywhere. Scotland has one of the best larders in the world and for chefs to appreciate that now is far better than it has ever been.

"The foodie revolution and online presence of writers has helped drive the changes. Everyone that sits in a restaurant is a critic these days. It's a new thing for everyone's critique to be made public, but that's good in a way. It all makes chefs aware that, what they are producing and what leaves their kitchen, is going to real people who are paying for it – it breaks down the barrier between the kitchen and the dining room.

"There's a consideration of wellbeing. When I was brought up in cooking there was a huge pot of demi-grand on the hob and that was the basis for most sauces, but gone are the big, gloopy, heavy sauces. People are trying to reduce the butters and cream they are cooking with, which is having an effect on what and how things are cooked. There is very little salt in cooking nowadays. So there are better cooking practices to be seen all round."

63

Fillet of Cod with a Pine Kernel Crust with Char Grilled Vegetables and Citrus Vinaigrette

55 Eastwoodmains Road
Giffnock
Glasgow G46 6PW
T: 0141 638 8422

- 6 x 200g Fillets of Cod
- 300g Fresh breadcrumbs
- 150g Pine kernels
- 50g Fresh chopped herbs
- 2 Oranges

- 2 Limes
- 2 Lemons
- 1kg Mixed charred vegetables
- Rapeseed oil
- Red wine vinegar

Crust
Saute pine kernels in a little butter, adding to breadcrumbs with the chopped herbs. Season with sea salt flakes and black pepper

Vinaigrette
Zest the fruits into a bowl, peel and segment. Squeeze excess juice into the bowl add vinegar and rapeseed oil

Cod
Place the cod on an oiled tray, cover with crust and bake in a pre-heated oven for 7-8mins at around 180-190°C Heat the chargrilled vegetables, then place onto a warm plate and top with the cod, spoon on zest, segments and vinaigrette

'Gerwegian,' Petra Wetzel now calls Glasgow home, but she will never forget her Bamastorff roots in Germany. After visiting Scotland as part of an exchange programme with Balfron High, Petra fell in love with Scotland, choosing to study at Glasgow University at 19 - the city became her adopted home and now she has brought a great slice of Germany to Glasgow's East End.

PETRA told us: "My family came to visit when I was studying and my dad asked why Glasgow didn't have a decent brewery. That got me thinking 'why didn't it' and then I started to think I could do it. But its not just a brewery back home, it's an experience and extension of a community. It's a brewery and food, with a bar and a place people can come to relax and socialise. That's what we have tried to do here – it's not twee, it's not Oktoberfest 365 days a year, or staff dressed in lederhosen. It's an authentic, back to basic approach of the German way.

"I think the food scene is going in the right direction now. It's nice to see such a huge variety now, there is a great amount of food available. When I came at first you had the choice of a Chinese, an Indian, or fish and chips. But now there is everything under the sun to choose from.

"Before West was born, people didn't think a German restaurant would work in Glasgow, but we have managed to change that opinion. It's difficult to replicate what we have done here. As much as our menu is noticeably German, the dishes aren't too different from well made gastro Scottish food. All our ingredients and produce are Scottish apart from our sausages, which we get shipped in from Germany. But the two cuisines are definitely complementary and Scotland has such a great natural larder to work with."

Venison and Munich Red Casserole

Templeton Building
Glasgow Green
Glasgow G40 1AW
T: 0141 550 0135

Casserole
- 1 kg Diced shoulder of venison
- 1 tsp Chopped garlic
- 1 tbsp Redcurrant jelly
- 1 tsp Tomato puree
- 6 Juniper berries
- 2 Bay leaves
- 1 Beef stock cube
- 2 pints WEST Munich Red Lager
- 2 tbsp Plain flour
- Thyme Bunch

Red Cabbage
- 1 Red cabbage
- 2 tbsp Redcurrant jelly
- 2 pints Red wine
- 200gm Caster sugar
- 1 Bay leaf
- 4 Juniper berries
- 1 Pint water

Potato Salad
- 1 kg New potatoes
- 1 Red onion
- 1 Small jar gherkins
- 2 tbsp Coarse grain mustard
- 3 tbsp Olive oil

First, flour the meat and fry all over in a hot saucepan. Once coloured, add in the garlic, bay leaves, juniper berries and tomato puree – stir well. Cover with the WEST Munich Red, top up with water if it isn't covered. Add in the stock cube and thyme. Bring to the boil and turn down to a simmer. Allow to cook for 1.5-2hrs until soft. Add the redcurrant jelly, this will dissolve into the casserole whilst thickening and sweetening it. Take off the stove and allow to cool.

Cut the cabbage into quarters and remove the core. Shred finely the cabbage and place in a saucepan. Add all the other ingredients to the pan and stir well. Bring to the boil and turn down to a simmer. Cook for two hours. Once the cabbage is soft, drain it through a colander with a bowl under it to catch the cooking liquid. Remove the bay leaf from the cabbage

Put the liquid back into the pan and reduce by at least half, this will thicken and get sticky. Put into a metal bowl and this can be used to decorate the plate when serving at the end. Allow to cool

Place the potatoes in a pan and cover with cold water, bring to the boil and cook until you can push a knife through the potatoes. Allow them to go cold, peel them and cut into half inch diced pieces. Peel the red onion and finely slice length ways. Cut the gherkins down the middle length ways, and slice thinly width ways. Add the onion, gherkins and oil to the potatoes along with the mustard. Season to taste and mix well.

Plating:
Using the red cabbage reduction saved earlier, drizzle across the plate for decorative effect and some sweetness. Spoon warm potato salad to one third of the plate. Do the same with the hot red cabbage on another third of the plate. In the remaining space, ladle the hot casserole up against the cabbage and potato, sprinkle with chives.

GLASGOW'S Southside is a beautiful area with fantastic history, and, like most suburbs of Glasgow, is just a stones throw from the city centre.

Now it has a beautiful stand-out restaurant to back up the natural surroundings. Ian Brown's in Giffnock opened in November 2010 following a full refurbishment and is a prime example of a good, modern, traditional Scottish restaurant.

With former Ubiquitous Chip head-chef, Ian at the helm and wife, Sheila operating front of house, food critics from all over Scotland have heralded the restaurant.

Many would say the quality of the food is better than anything else you'll find in the Southside, and they'd be right, but it is the homely clench embracing you as you enter that makes the venue such a success.

The menu is traditionally Scottish with a good mix of fish and game meats, as well as traditional beef, pork and chicken dishes. There are also stunning vegetarian options on offer.

The Eastwoodmains property offers culinary thrills and is definitely worth venturing out of the city for.

WHO would have thought you could set up a Bavarian brewery in the East End of Glasgow and establish yourself as one of the most talked about places in the city?

Not many, but Petra Wetzel has done it with a charm, success, and a character second to none.

Set in the old Templeton building on Glasgow Green, WEST Brewery is one of the most honest ventures available in Glasgow today.

The beautiful architecture outside is continued inside, where a traditional German design offers great comfort to a very vast space. A grand piano, sturdy wooden furniture, a huge bar and views of the on-site brewery help fill the huge space, but you'll never feel cramped.

Great German beer is matched with great German food using the best of Scottish produce – except their sausages, which are imported from Germany – with the Munich-style beer hall serving up spectacular dishes such as a St. Mungo lager-battered fish and chips, jäger schnitzel, currywurst, and of course, Munich Red venison stew.

WEST is an ideal place for a candle lit dinner, group meal, and family function, offering charming service, fine food and fantastic beer.

CAMERON House on the banks of Loch Lomond is surely one of the finest experiences any tourist or city slicker looking to get away for the weekend could hope to enjoy.

Looking out to the bonnie banks, visitors will love the splendour of their surroundings. That splendour continues in the surroundings of the Cameron Grill and it continues further still with the quality of food on offer.

A restaurant that serves the best Scottish produce, Executive Chef, Ryan Neill uses that produce to present some truly astonishing dishes. This is modern Scottish culinary excellence at the top of its game.

A fascinating mural depicting rogues, thieves and vagabonds from clan days gone by, adorns the walls of the contemporary restaurant, with a palpable anticipation of what's to come brewing from the sights, sounds, and smells coming from the open plan kitchen.

The salmon bar, offers up the finest smoked and cured salmon, including the chef's own beetroot, honey and Glengoyne whisky cured version. And as if the anticipation wasn't enough, a walk in wine cellar heightens the expectations and excitement of diners.

An a la carte menu made up of Scotland's finest fish, beef, pork, game and lamb, Cameron House is a true first class dining experience.

67

THIS book is about Glasgow and the West, but it is also about showcasing how Scotland's food scene has moved forward.

One area we have made huge steps forward in is the food available at hotels. No longer are restaurants there the by-product or afterthought of a large chain – indeed, they can be the epicentre of some of our best food.

Such a place is Forest Hills in Aberfoyle, just 26 miles from Glasgow. A stunning hotel and scenery is matched by a stunning restaurant that serves up first class food.

The Garden Restaurant is traditionally decorated, serving up food that showcases a combination of both classic and contemporary fayre. Dishes here can be rich and elegant, showcasing the best of Scotland's larder - such as beef and game.

But the gentle touch and appreciation of finer, more delicate produce and flavours by Head Chef David Robertson is also showcased, highlighting a side of Scotland's larder and palate often forgotten.

A fine example of what to expect when you step away from the city and suburbia, Forest Hills offers a chance to relax and enjoy the best of Scottish style and comfort in beautiful surroundings.

Ryan Neill is the executive chef at Cameron House, one of Scotland's foremost exclusive venues. The five-star resort plays a massive part in showcasing the very best of everything Scottish throughout the year and that's something Ryan is proud of. He said: "We're a Scottish restaurant and we sell Scottish produce. That's the way it should be and I think it makes a big difference."

A Tasting of Cairnhill Farm Beef Fillet, Oxtail Cannelloni & Bone Marrow Gratin

Loch Lomond
Alexandria
Dunbartonshire
G83 8QZ
T: 0871 222 4681

- 1 Centre Cut Beef fillet (1.1kg) all fat removed
- 1 Medium oxtail
- 500g Beef shin
- Bottle of deep red wine
- 500g Red Rooster potatoes
- 10 Banana shallots
- 12 Cherry tomatoes
- 4 Large carrots
- 500g Baby leaf spinach
- Bulb of garlic
- 2 Sprigs of thyme
- 2ltr dark chicken stock

- 250ml red wine sauce
- 100g Unsalted butter
- 25g Micro herbs

For the Pasta Dough
- 180g of 00 pasta flour
- 2 Egg yolks
- ½ tsp Salt
- 100g Cooked puréed spinach drained of excess water
- Salt and pepper
- 100ml Double cream
- 50g Parmesan grated
- 50g Fresh breadcrumbs

Method:

Place oxtail in red wine, adding ½ of garlic bulb and the thyme. Cover and marinade for 24 hours. Next day, warm chicken stock and place to one side. In a medium to hot pan sear off oxtail then allow to cool. Place oxtail in a deep tray and cover with marinade and chicken stock. Cover well and place tinfoil over the tray. Cook in a pre-heated oven at 120°C for four hours, turning and checking after the first two hours.

Soak the bone marrow in brine to allow marrow to be cleaned and easily removed from the bone. Once soaked, remove and pat dry with a cloth. Chop marrow into inch cubes and place to one side.

While the oxtail is cooking make pasta dough. In a food processor mix together flour and eggs. Pulse until mixture becomes like breadcrumbs. Add the salt and cooked spinach, then pulse again until mixed together. Remove and knead together until completely together. Cling film and rest in the fridge until required.

Wrap beef fillet tightly in cling film until it forms a sausage shape, refrigerate until needed.

For the shallot garnishes, roughly chop five shallots and sweat down in butter and a clove of garlic without colouring. Add a splash of cream and cook out for a few minutes, then blitz shallots in a juicer until silky smooth.

Take two shallots, skin on, and cut lengthways in half. Roast in a hot oven until soft and juicy.

Slice remaining shallots into rings, lightly coat in flour then deep fry until crisp.

Once cooked, remove oxtail and flake down all the meat from the bone. Once flaked down, reduce cooking liquor until a sauce like consistency. In a saucepan, sweat off a small brunoise of carrot and shallot then add the sauce. Pour all over the oxtail. Roll pasta dough using a pasta machine at the thinnest setting. Cut into long rectangles, then blanch in boiling water for a minute. Refresh in ice cold water, dry and place aside. Warm the oxtail and place a 50g amount into the pasta, then roll up into a sausage shape ensuring all ends are trimmed and pasta is sealed.

Lightly dust the marrow with seasoned flour and pan fry until coloured on each side. Now add to the remaining oxtail, mix well and add into the mini pie dishes. Top the mix with duchess potato, then sprinkle with parmesan cheese and breadcrumbs. Gratinate in a hot oven for 12mins.

Before cooking, remove beef fillet, bringing to room temperature. Pan fry in vegetable oil and butter. Cook in a preheated oven at 170°C for 20mins. If using a meat thermometer probe the meat to 45-48°C for medium rare, or cook to your liking.

Plate up by creating two drags of the smooth purée, the pink beef topped with smoked Maldon sea salt to the left. The marrow gratin at the top of the plate. Place some wilted spinach on the right hand side then top with reheated oxtail cannelloni. This can be reheated in a bamboo steamer. Garnish with two roasted cherry tomatoes, confit shallot, crispy shallot rings and a drizzle of red wine sauce. Sprinkle with some micro herbs.

David Robertson at Macdonald Forest Hills Hotel & Spa

AS much as I enjoy exploring the culinary offerings of other cultures, you really can't beat a proper home cooked classic. Scottish reared beef, combined with simple vegetables and a lovely red wine jus, hits the spot every time. Beef cheeks are an underused cut but shouldn't be overlooked. Quite literally the cheek of the cow, it's a really flavoursome interesting cut that, when cooked properly, can be beautifully tender. It also produces a really rich and clear gravy that adds depth to the jus.

Slowly braised beef cheek with creamed potatoes, greens and red wine jus

MACDONALD FOREST HILLS HOTEL & SPA
Kinlochard, The Trossachs, Aberfoyle
Stirlingshire FK8 3TL
T: 0844 879 9057

- 2 Beef cheeks
- 2 Bay leaf
- Fresh rosemary
- Fresh thyme
- ½ Bulb garlic
- ½ Glass of red wine
- 1 tsp Tomato paste
- 600g Fresh chicken stock

- 600g Fresh veal stock
- 1 Carrot
- 1 Stick celery
- 1 Large onion
- Salt and pepper
- Olive oil
- Small knob of cold butter

Preheat oven to 150°C

Trim your beef cheeks (your butcher can help do this) season and caramelise in olive oil. Place in a deep casserole dish.

Caramelise carrots, celery, and garlic, add the red wine, tomato paste and herbs then add stocks and add to casserole dish.

Cover with tin foil, place in oven and braise for about 6-8 hours or until meat starts to fall apart. Remove beef cheeks and reserve.

Pass the liquid through a fine sieve and reduce liquor to required consistency.

To Serve

Make some creamed potatoes and pipe into a bowl. Blanch some shredded buttered greens and place on top of creamed potatoes. Warm beef cheek and place on garnish.

Heat sauce and add cold knob of butter to give the sauce a rich flavour and pour over beef.

Asummer staple, salads are light and refreshing, and can be prepared in advance for ease when enjoying a lazy lunch in the sunshine. This unusual salad combines some fantastic Scottish flavours – luxurious smoked salmon, fresh haddock – with delicate herbs and summery vegetables. Don't be tempted to plump for a shop bought pickle, taking the extra time to prepare the homemade pickled cucumber is well worth it as the refreshing, zingy flavours will be unrivalled. The addition of a modern twist on the classic Scotch egg is a real crowd pleaser, with dainty quails eggs complemented perfectly by the haddock mousse and crispy panko breadcrumbs. Take time over presentation to really wow your guests – this is a pretty dish that deserves a little more attention. Enjoy in the sunshine with a glass of dry white wine.

Scottish smoked salmon, pickled cucumber & haddock scotch quails egg

73

**MACDONALD FOREST
HILLS HOTEL & SPA**
Kinlochard, The Trossachs,
Aberfoyle
Stirlingshire FK8 3TL
T: 0844 879 9057

- 400g Smoked salmon
- 1 Cucumber
- Sprig of thyme
- Sprig of rosemary
- Mixed cress
- 60ml Double cream
- Small bunch of coriander
- Small bunch of parsley
- Small bunch of dill
- 1 Haddock fillet

- 6 Quail's eggs
- 2 Slices of white bread, crusts off
- 1 Lemon and lime
- 50g Chinese panko breadcrumbs
- Rock salt
- 180ml White wine vinegar
- 150g Caster sugar

To make the pickling, bring sugar, white wine vinegar, thyme and rosemary to the boil and put aside. Peel off cucumber skin and with remaining cucumber, peel long strips with potato peeler. Add to warm pickling liquor.

Boil eggs for two minutes in boiling water. Cool quickly in cold water. Once cool, peel carefully as they will be soft. Set aside.

To make mousse, put haddock, lemon and lime, sliced bread, 20g panko breadcrumbs, salt and herbs into food processor and blitz to a rough pulp. Slowly add cream until you have a sausage-meat like consistency. Set aside.

To make the Scotch egg, weigh out 35g of mousse and carefully mould around the peeled quails egg. Roll quickly in panko breadcrumbs and set in fridge for one hour. Then, cook scotch quail egg for three minutes by shallow frying in submerged sunflower oil until golden brown. Reserve for use.

To assemble, arrange salmon in middle of plate. Place pickled cucumber in middle of salmon, with mixed cress. Carefully cut egg in half and place on top of cress. Sprinkle rock salt on yolk. Serve and enjoy

RACHNA Dheer, Babu Kitchen: "The Glasgow food scene is going in the right direction. There are more and more new fusion places opening up, offering authentic food but more with an interesting Scottish twist. We have a great larder here and it makes sense to provide authentic food that is not tapered to Western market, but that still makes the most of that produce. Fusion is about marrying the two cultures, not alienating anyone.

"So if someone comes to us asking for a soup, I can offer them a lentil soup, but use a daal base with lovely spicing. The food scene is not just trained chefs anymore, striving for fine dining. It's travelled, younger chefs, who have different training and different experiences. And you can see that here in Glasgow with a great combination of different cultures in the food available.

"Bombay and Scottish food marry very well. The vegetables and spices work really well together. We do a bacon chapati wrap, which is a take on a BLT, and that's a good way of showcasing the mix. We use a red chilli and garlic mayo, served with fresh coriander, chilli, diced onions and then bacon.

"Street food is the way forward, I think you'll see a lot more of that kind of food in the next year or so. There are so many in Glasgow just now as well. You have us, Fire in Babylon, Smoak, the Street Food Cartel guys – it's a really exciting time.

"More and more now there are events and opportunities to showcase our produce and the food scene in Glasgow as a whole."

186 West Regent Street
Glasgow G2 4RU
T: 0141 204 4042

Aviyal (Keralan coconutty veggies)

- 1 Butternut squash
- 1 Turnip
- 4 Medium carrots
- 3 tsps Jeera (cumin)

- 25g Green chillies with seeds
- 12 Kadi Patta (curry leaves)
- 250g Shredded coconut
- 2 tbsp Oil

De-seed butternut squash and cut into inch thick slices. Cut the carrots and turnip in inch thick slices, so they all are match stick length. Sprinkle all the veg with a tablespoon of oil and place in the oven at gas mark five until al dente. Grind shredded coconut, green chilli and cumin with 100g of water to make into a paste. Heat oil, add Kadi Patta and sauté for a minute. Add ground coconut spice paste, sauté, and sea salt. Add the veg and cook for two minutes. Serve sprinkled with chopped coriander and lime juice.

REVIEW

GLASGOW'S street food scene is finally up and running and there are some fine examples of global cuisine.

One such example is the Babu Bombay Street Kitchen run by Rachna Dheer and Gail Finlayson. Starting off as a small-scale tiffin service, the buzz and excitement surrounding the fayre on offer was all positive.

Now in their small and quaint West Regent Street premises, Rachna and Gail are serving up top Indian snacks in surroundings ideal for those looking to grab something fresh, innovative, and authentic on the go.

With a range of original sandwiches and wraps using bread, puris, rotis, they also offer snack pots made up of rice and curry, or 'dahl of the day'. And for those all caffeined out, real chai is available almost on tap.

Authentic ingredients and flavours offer up explosive combinations for what is truly delightful food.

Brian Austin of Fire in Babylon shared Glasgow's food scene and his thoughts on the street food scene.

He said: "The food scene in Glasgow is definitely more varied than it was a few years ago. From a punter's point of view it's easier to go and find new dishes to try. It's also easier to find ingredients meaning people can have a go at creating new dishes at home.

"New things are always exciting and I think street food can fall into that category. In terms of demand, I think the demand is there simply because people like to eat and be outside. I would say the scene here is still in it's early days and,

whilst it's not that easy to be a vendor, it's great for the punter because the emphasis is on quality and originality and not so much on just making money.

"West Indian culture and food is its own thing and whilst there are some things that overlap with the Scottish larder, we would never try to make it into something it isn't. Having said that, we live in Scotland and some of the food here is amazing, so naturally we have come up with a couple of fusion dishes. The most popular one is probably the jerk venison stew."

Doubles

A lot of people think of jerk when they think of the West Indies but Doubles is thee street food of Trinidad and Tobago. Vendors would normally be at the side of the road as people make their way to work in the morning and again as they make their way home in the evening.
For this dish you need to do three things. Make the dough, make the curry, fry the dough. To save time, make the dough first and whilst it is proving, make the curry. Once the dough is ready, fry it off and then simply spoon the curry over it.

For the dough:
• 450g Flour
• 1 tsp Turmeric powder
• 1 tbsp Baking powder
• 1 tsp Yeast
• ¼ tsp Sugar
• 1 tsp Salt
• 1 ½ Cups water

• 1 tbsp Oil
• Oil for frying

For the Channa:
• 2 tins Channa/chickpeas
• 2 tsp Baking soda
• 2 tbsp Oil
• 1 tsp Curry powder

• 1 tsp Turmeric
• 1 tsp Geera (cumin)
• 1 tsp Masala
• 2 Cloves finely chopped garlic
• ½ Onion, finely chopped
• 5 Chadon beni leaves (or coriander), finely chopped
• Salt and pepper to taste

Dough:
In a cup, mix the yeast and sugar and add a little lukewarm water. The yeast should activate after a few minutes and the liquid will become frothy. Whilst waiting for that to happen, get a bowl and add the flour, turmeric powder, baking powder and salt.
Once the yeast mixture is nice and frothy, add it to the flour.
Using your hands mix everything together.
Add the remaining two cups of water bit by bit until the mixture no longer sticks to the side of the bowl.
If the mixture is too wet, add a little more flour.
Once you have a nice mixture, pour a little oil over the top of it, cover with a dishcloth and set somewhere warm to prove.
After about 40mins the doughs should have risen.

Channa:
Basically, you want to make a simple little chickpea curry. Get a saucepan and gently heat a large spoonful of oil or ghee. Add the curry powder to the oil to activate some of the flavours.
Try to use a madras curry powder as it's closest to the ones we have at home.
After a couple of minutes, add the onion and fry gently till they become translucent and soft. At this stage you want to add the garlic, ginger and chickpeas.
Keep stirring so nothing sticks or burns. Add the

cumin, turmeric and coriander. You will want to start gradually adding a little bit of the stock to keep the chickpeas nice and moist. Season with salt and pepper and cook till the chickpeas are soft.
If the curry is too liquid at the end of cooking, just take a spoon and mash up some of the chickpeas. This will thicken the sauce.

Frying the dough:
Pinch off a golf ball sized piece of dough and set on an oiled cooking tray.
Repeat till you have enough of these.
Get a saucepan, pour about an inch of oil and heat till it's hot enough to fry.
Make sure you have a little oil on your hands
Using your finger tips and thumbs flatten the golf balls till they are like mini pizza doughs. Keep them thin.
Fry in the oil, should take only about a minute.
Remove from oil and wrap up in a warm dish cloth – this is important as it helps the doubles bread to stay soft and light.
Repeat till you have enough of these.

The reason a doubles is called a doubles is because it consists of two pieces of double bread. Once you have your doubles bread fried off, put two on a plate and spoon some curry over it. You don't want to cover all the bread, just about two thirds of it.
Finally, add a little pepper sauce or some cucumber and coriander relish and you are in business.

77

ROSS from Cafezique told us: "The mackerel and beetroot pate is almost an ever present at Cafezique on our lunch and dinner menu. Five years on, it's still very popular with regular and new customers alike. It's great as a light lunch or smaller as a starter at dinner.

"The pate can be made the day you are eating, although we would recommend making a day or two in advance. It is very simple to make, especially with a food processor, although a chunkier version can be made with just your hands and a knife. At the cafe we serve it with toasted Delizique seeded wholemeal bread, dressed organic leaves and flowers from Arran."

Smoked mackerel & beetroot pate

66 Hyndland Street
Glasgow G11 5PT
T: 0141 339 7180

- 4 Ready smoked mackerel fillets (or smoke your own over oak chips)
- 2 Cooked beetroot
- 125g Cream cheese

- 2 tsp Horseradish
- ½ tsp Garlic
- ½ Lemon zest
- 4 tsp Olive oil
- 1 Handful chopped parsley

Remove skin and any bones from mackerel. With a spoon carefully remove the bloodline (dark brown flesh) from under the skin.
Add all ingredients to a food processor. Blend until smooth and place in fridge to set approx 1 hour at least.

WITH its own deli right next door you can rest assured quality ingredients matter at Cafezique.

Seasonal, fresh, high quality ingredients are used to produce simple yet stunning dishes to great effect. Cafezique offers a wide variety of choice to cater to all needs and tastes, whatever the time of day.

Diners can take advantage of the cafe's reputation for the best breakfast around all day, or they can take the conventional route and tuck into the equally delicious lunch and dinner options.

Confident, stylish cooking makes the most of the fresh produce available and makes this a place you'll want to go to again.

Floor to ceiling windows give a spacious, airy feeling throughout, even when dining on the mezzanine level, and the relaxed atmosphere adds to the experience.

Indeed, Cafezique is a popular drinks venue for locals in the know, with the beer and wine selection proving popular with stylish professionals of the area.

And for those who fancy a bit of indulgence in their lives, the cakes and bakes on offer at both Delizique and Cafezique are not to be missed.

IT may be tucked away in a business park, but Up on the Hill is one of Glasgow's most exciting cafes serving up some of the finest breakfasts, lunches and small plate meals around.

Topped off with fantastic coffee, great music, and friendly service with good chat, this is a must visit place.

The tasty, hearty food is made up using only the freshest, quality ingredients. A fine range of sandwiches, burgers and salads has satisfied regulars since opening and continues to captivate old and new diners.

And if it's not the food that initially grabs your attention, the spectacular vista over Glasgow is one of the best around, and will captivate any visitor.

With large windows showcasing the Campsies, the balcony also serves up a fine location for al fresco dining, making the most of the good weather – when it's here.

This is a great hangout offering fine food with a fine view. Hopefully this well kept secret is well out the bag.

Niall Holmes, Up on The Hill Cafe:

I think the food scene is brilliant here just now. There is a huge onus on sustainability and locality, which is seeing a return of the cottage industry, where small companies are getting a look in. Small produce like Dunlop Cheese is all of a sudden famous again and that's fantastic. There is a real name checking of the produce we are using and it's great to see.

"What's struck me recently is the variety on offer. The big thing about going through a recession is that the end product now is a product of genuine originality. People have started out and done their own thing, they've moved away from the chain culture. It's almost gone full circle in that respect. It's small, local, independent ventures. There's no longer this insipid desire for chain restaurants. That's the way of it elsewhere, like Berlin for instance.

"The Internet has made the world such a small place - countries aren't so far away anymore and it's easier to use different cultural concepts, ingredients and recipes. You no longer want for anything when you're shopping for food or out eating now. You can get just about any ingredients from across the world you want. Whether it's Lupe Pinto's on Great Western Road, or whether it's the supermarket, you can get ingredients now you just wouldn't have been able to get a few years ago. That's a good thing, but then everyone quickly becomes an expert. You can't get away with as much and it has driven up the customer's expectation – it keeps our standards high though and stops complacency."

Niall & Dudley

Bunny Chow Chicken Methi

2A Eagle Street
Glasgow G4 9XA
T: 0141 333 0303

- 4 tbsp Groundnut oil
- 1 Large red onion, finely chopped
- 2 Garlic cloves, crushed
- 1 in Fresh ginger, peeled and finely grated
- 700g Boneless, skinless chicken thigh or breast, cut into 2½ cm chunks
- 8 tbsp Fresh finely chopped tomatoes

- 1 tbsp Tomato puree
- 3 Green chillies, finely chopped
- 1 tsp Turmeric
- ¼ tsp Chilli powder
- 1 tsp Garam masala
- 2 tbsp Dried fenugreek leaves (Qasuri Methi)
- Round loaf, for serving

Set a wok over a medium heat adding oil when hot. Add the red onion and fry until light brown, then add garlic and ginger. Fry a further two minutes. Add chicken, browning for two minutes. Add tomatoes and chillies and stir for two minutes, then add turmeric and ½ tsp of salt.

Mix well for five minutes before adding chilli powder and garam masala. Stir, then crumble in dried fenugreek leaves.

Mix in enough water just to cover chicken (about 350 ml) and bring to a simmer. Cover and cook over a low heat for 30mins.

Take a round loaf – I recommend a sour dough cob – cut a lid from the top, pull the dough from the main part till hollow and fill with the chicken methi.

Serve, with optional toppings of chutney, raita or pickles.

Ayrshire

Executive Chef of Cochrane Inn and Highgrove House Hotel, Lesley McQuiston:

AS a chef you want to use fresh and local produce, hence having passionate and high quality suppliers in and around our local area makes creation of seasonal menus and specials a pleasure to develop and work with. From Freshly caught Seafood delivered daily to extra mature Ayrshire beef, the possibilities are endless here. I am very grateful to have all of this available right on the doorstep of the kitchen.

"With some of the talents emerging through the Ayrshire hospitality trade, combined with the top end level of produce available in our local area, Ayrshire is fast becoming as well renowned as some of our big city rivals.

"I think Scotland and Ayrshire need to show that we're just as good as everywhere else, if not better. We have got the produce and we've got the amenities – Ayrshire is up there with the best.

"We have one of the best views in Ayrshire, looking out over Arran. Nothing compares to the view and people come specifically for that – we have our regulars and we know where to sit them and why."

Sage 'n' Leek Scotch Egg, with Whisky Mayo

High Maybole Road
Alloway
Ayrshire KA7 4PQ
T: 01292 442466

Scotch Egg
- 4 Large free-range eggs
- 275g Sausage meat
- 1 tsp Fresh sage leaves
- 1 tbsp Chopped fresh parsley
- 1 Leek very finely chopped
- Salt and freshly ground black pepper
- 125g Plain flour, seasoned with salt and ground black pepper
- 1 Free-range egg, beaten
- 125g Breadcrumbs
- Vegetable oil, for deep frying

Whisky Mayonnaise
- 290ml Groundnut oil
- 2 Eggs, yolks only
- 1 Garlic clove, crushed
- 1 Heaped tsp of powdered mustard
- 1 Level tsp of salt
- Milled black pepper
- 1 tsp white wine vinegar
- 1 Shot of good quality whisky
- A pinch of cayenne pepper

Method for Scotch Egg
Place eggs in a pan of cold salted water over a high heat and bring to the boil. Reduce heat and simmer for nine minutes. Drain and cool eggs under cold running water and peel.

Mix sausage meat with sage, parsley and leek in a bowl and season with salt and freshly ground pepper.

Divide sausage meat into four and flatten each out on a clean surface into ovals.

Place seasoned flour onto a plate and cover each boiled egg with the flour.

Place an egg onto the centre of each sausage oval and wrap around the egg completely.

Dip each scotch egg into the beaten egg and then roll in the breadcrumbs to completely cover.

Heat oil in a deep pan until a breadcrumb sizzles when dropped in.

Carefully place each scotch egg into the oil and deep fry for 8-10mins until golden and crisp, ensuring the sausage meat is completely cooked. Carefully remove from the oil and drain on kitchen paper.

Method for Mayonnaise
Put egg yolks into a bowl and add crushed garlic, mustard powder, cayenne pepper, salt and freshly milled black pepper – mix all the ingredients together well.

Using an electric mixer in one hand, slowly add the groundnut oil a drop at a time until the mixture thickens.

At this point add a teaspoon of vinegar to thin down the mixture.

Continue mixing and adding the groundnut oil in a steady stream until all the oil had been added.

Taste and add more salt and pepper as required. Finally add in the whisky and mix well.

Apple Tarte Tatin

Old Loans Road
Troon
Ayrshire KA10 7HL
T: 01292 312511

- 50g Unsalted butter, cut into cubes, plus more for greasing
- 4 Sheets of ready-made puff pastry
- 6 Granny Smith apples

- 100g Caster sugar
- 1 Vanilla Pod
- Icing sugar, for dusting
- To serve – Vanilla ice cream and caramel springs

Preheat the oven to 230°C / 450°F / Gas 8
Line the base of four individual 10cm round tatin pans / baking tins with rounds of baking paper. Grease paper with a little butter.
Roll puff pastry into circles about 10cm in diameter and 2mm thick.
Peel, core and cut apples into quarters.
Heat caster sugar with two tablespoons of water and vanilla pod seeds in a heavy-based saucepan and cook gently until caramel light gold colour.
Remove from heat and add cubed butter, stirring well.
Pour a thin layer of caramel on the base of each lined tatin pan or tin. Pack the apple quarters in a circular pattern on top of the caramel.
Drape a circle of pastry over the top, then tuck it in well to completely encase the apple. Leave to rest in

a cool place for 20mins so pastry won't shrink when it goes in the oven.
Dust each circle of pastry with a little icing sugar, put in oven and bake for 18-20mins, or until pastry is golden brown and apples soft.
Remove tartes from oven and leave to rest for one minute, allowing the caramel to cool and set slightly. Remember hot caramel burns the skin badly, so be careful when you turn out your tartes.
To do so, place a dessert plate over the top of each pan and, with a twist of the wrist, carefully flip pan and plate over so tarte ends up apple-side upwards, on the plate. Remove the paper.
Use remainder of vanilla pod to garnish top of tart and serve with a scoop of vanilla ice cream on top and some caramel springs. Dust the whole plate with icing sugar.

SITUATED on the infamous medieval bridge in Rabbie Burns' final verse of Tam O Shanter, the Brig o'Doon is a place of historical and literary significance to Scotland.

Now a first class resort and shining light in the Costley portfolio, Brig o'Doon is a place of culinary significance to Scotland too.

Renowned for its imaginative and mouthwatering selection of traditional dishes, Brig o'Doon serves up one of the finest examples of Scottish food using the very best of local produce.

And the restaurant continues to showcase the best of Scottish, drawing on the literary influences nearby to provide an all year round Burns Supper menu.

In an ode to Burns character Tam, the 'Witches and Warlocks Room,' with its high ceiling and panoramic window, can be utilised for private functions whilst offering an intimate, candlelit atmosphere.

Diners can enjoy panoramic views over the stunning gardens and flowing River Doon, and can satisfy their sweet tooth with ice cream or coffee from the Banks O Doon Coffee Shop.

HEADED up by Executive Chef, Lesley McQuiston, Highgrove House Hotel is another gem in the Costley crown.

With stunning views over the Irish sea, the venue is ideally placed on the outskirts of the idyllic Troon, providing diners the tranquillity needed to enjoy the sights, scents and tastes of the stunning a la carte menu.

But as well as the high end dining on offer, there is something for everyone here at the refurbished Highgrove, with hearty Scottish breakfasts, lunches, suppers and fine dinners all catered for.

And, with such a wealth of natural produce on its Ayrshire doorstep, chef Lesley is somewhat spoilt for choice as to what to prepare.

Thankfully the menu reflects the best of Scotland's, and indeed Ayrshire's, larder. The kitchen brigade strive to provide interesting, tasty food with daily specials using the season's specialities in delicious ways.

Seafood is always available on the menu, with locally landed fish arriving on the premises daily. Their dedicated grill section tempts the palate of guests who enjoy mouthwatering steaks.

And the homemade puddings are a must when dining at Highgrove, especially the Costley ice creams.

SINCE taking over this stunning venue in 1989, the Costley family have worked tirelessly to ensure Lochgreen House Hotel is the number one offering in their portfolio.

Now serving up a stunning selection of dishes and fine wine to accompany, it could be said the job is very much done – however, that won't see this brigade resting on their laurels.

Staff here continue to provide a first class experience, showcasing the best of Scottish dining.

Set in the stunning Tapestry Restaurant, menus offer a real taste of Scotland's larder, with the kitchen staff using the best of methods to bring the best out of the raw ingredients. That includes an abundance of local seafood, meat, game and cheese available in Ayrshire.

Eating here is a true experience, where diners can enjoy a variety of both modern and classical dishes prepared with imagination and flair by Andrew Costley and his team.

Lochgreen House Hotel is one of the finest restaurants in Ayrshire and its three AA Red Rosette awards and continued desire to improve are testament to that.

The personal supervision of Executive Chef Andrew ensures every meal is prepared and served to the highest international standards.

AFTER a five year spell in the wilderness without a pub, the people of Kirkmichael were rewarded for their patience in 2012 with the return of the Kirkmichael Arms – and then some.

The existing restaurant area was increased, but the friendly atmosphere and traditional character remained. And with the kitchen also expanding in the refurbishment, the people of Kirkmichael have gained one of Ayrshire's finest gastro pubs.

That's thank to the appointment of Ewan McAllister as Head Chef - with him at the helm, diners are getting a true dining experience with fine modern, technical dishes, showcasing the best of Scottish produce.

Lunches and evening meals can be chosen from the extensive menu, and are supported by a daily specials board and comforting home baking. The bar even showcases local craft beers and ales from the Ayr Brewing Company, as well as a selection of malts.

A fantastic offering in the heart of Ayrshrie, the refurbished Kirkmichael Arms has kept its 'pub in the country' feel, with slate flooring, charming wood burning stove and fireplace as its centre piece.

Here, faces new and old are given a warm welcome upon arrival, and are treated as Royalty during their stay.

Seared Orkney Scallops, Pak Choi, Carrot Salad, Sesame and Carrot Puree

Monktonhill Road
Southwood, Troon
Ayrshire KA10 7EN
T: 01292 313 343

- 4 Large Orkney scallops
- 2 Pak choi

Carrot puree ingredients:
- 2 Large cooked carrots
- 2 tbsp Sesame seeds
- 1 tbsp Sesame seed oil
- 15g Butter
- 1 tbsp Lemon juice
- 75ml Double cream

Warm carrot salad ingredients:
- 1 Carrot
- 1 tsp Sesame seed oil
- 1 Squeezed orange
- 5g Butter

Veloute Ingredients:
- 150ml Fish stock
- 50ml Coconut milk
- 25g Mango chutney
- 1 Garlic clove, finely chopped
- 10g Freshly grated ginger
- 5g Lemongrass paste
- ½ tsp Cumin
- ½ tsp Chili powder
- ½ tsp Madras curry powder
- 250ml Double cream
- 1 Lime leaf

Cleaning scallops

Rinse scallops under cool running water and pat dry. Check over the scallops as you're handling them and remove the side-muscle if you find any still attached.

Carrot puree

Place the peeled and diced carrots in a pan with sesame oil, seeds and butter, then cook without colour, place lid on top and simmer for 10mins or until carrots are well cooked.

Add the cream and lemon juice before bringing the mix back to the boil, then remove from heat and season to taste. Place carrot mix in a food processor and blend thoroughly till smooth.

Warm carrot salad

Use a mandalin or a peeler to finely cut the carrot. Place the remaining ingredients together with the carrots in a sauce pan and cook over a gentle heat until al dente.

Veloute

Place fish stock in pan reducing by half. Fry garlic, ginger and lemongrass paste, add the mango chutney, cumin, chili, madras curry powder, lime leaf and reduced fish stock.

Finish with coconut milk and cream, leaving to infuse for 20mins then pass through muslin or fine sieve.

Scallops

Heat a non stick pan and add one teaspoon of olive oil. Season scallops with salt and pepper and add to the pan, searing for 2-3 minutes until golden brown. Turn scallops and add 15g of butter, basting them with the now nut brown butter for an additional minute.

EWAN McAllister, head chef, said: "The more people coming to Scotland the better. We are a small countryside operator, so we need to make sure we are different and stand out from the rest. We use a lot of local produce, with our meat, venison, fish all being as local as possible.

"We are trying to produce high quality food and a modern take on some favourites, as well as freshening up the presentation. You don't just want to see everything slapped onto the plate.

"The food scene has changed massively. There is a lot more attention to detail needed - you can't get away with mediocre anymore and that's a good thing.

"The dish is something we have on a lot at the weekends and it's very popular. It showcases the best of what we do and the best of produce. Our meat comes from a family farm and the quality is second to none – I'm not sure you'd get better anywhere else."

Drumore Farm (Kirkmichael) Piétrian Pork

3-5 Straiton Road
Kirkmichael KA19 7PH
T: 01655 750200

- 1 Pork belly
- 1 Pigs head
- 4 Garlic cloves
- 1 Cauliflower
- 1 Bunch of Thyme
- 1 Bag of baby spinach
- 4 Bay leaves
- 2 Langoustines
- Small bunch of parsley
- 2 Large Maris Piper potatoes

- 50ml Red wine jus
- 1 tbsp Horseradish sauce
- 1 Egg
- Butter
- Flour
- Salt
- 100g Panko breadcrumbs
- 4 Slices of Serrano ham
- 1pt Milk
- Vegetable oil

Pigs Head

Use gas torch to remove any excess hair. Bone out head, trim excess fat and place in small roasting tray. Cover with vegetable oil, put two cloves of smashed garlic, two bay leaves, sprig of thyme and cover with tin foil, cook at 140°C for 4 to 4½ hours until tender.

Lift out and pick through meat carefully, keeping in good sized pieces. Remove garlic from confit oil, puree and add to head meat. Chop and add parsley – no seasoning required.

Place cling film on table, lay out Serrano ham on cling film, put head meat at one end and roll tightly – place in fridge and allow to set.

Pork Belly

Trim excess fat, season with salt and place in a roasting tray. Cover with vegetable oil, place some bay leaves, thyme and garlic in the oil. Cover with foil and cook in oven at 130°C for 4½ hours until completely tender. Remove from oil and place between two trays with heavy weight on top, press in fridge overnight. Trim ends and cut into portion sizes.

Cauliflower Purée

Cut into florets and simmer gently with ½ milk, ½ water until soft. Remove and purée until smooth,

season with salt to taste.

Langoustines

Drop into fast boiling water and remove straight away into ice water. Remove tail meat and chill in fridge.

Horseradish Potatoes

Bake potatoes in oven until cooked, remove flesh from skin and press through drum sieve. Add horseradish and salt to taste. Roll into small balls, chill then panni (flour, egg and panko breadcrumbs).

Assemble

Pan sear pork belly with small sprig of thyme and butter in medium heat until golden brown and crisp. Season with salt and set aside, keep warm.

Warm cauliflower purée. Pan fry one slice of pigs head until crispy and set aside, keep warm.

Sauté the langoustine tails in butter gently taking care not to colour, set aside.

Cook potato balls in fryer at 170°C for four minutes until golden brown and crisp.

Gently wilt spinach, season with salt and drain excess water.

Warm plate, place cauliflower puree across middle of plate, arrange different elements to dish, finish off with a small drizzle of red wine jus.

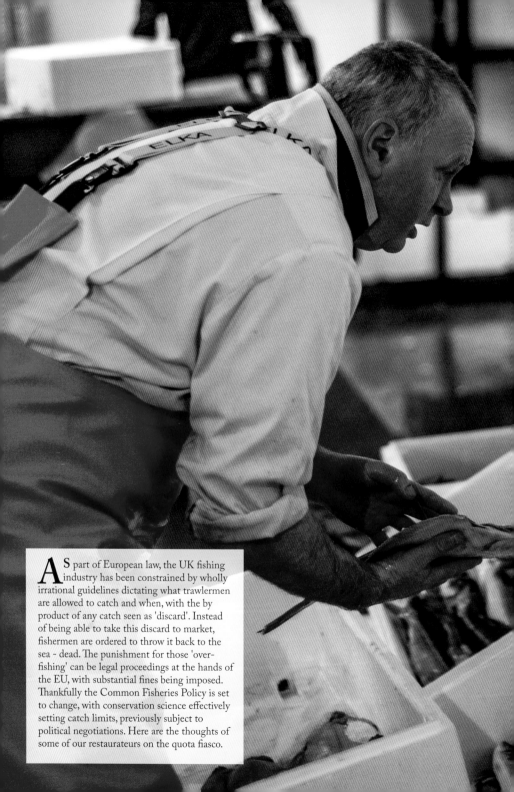

AS part of European law, the UK fishing industry has been constrained by wholly irrational guidelines dictating what trawlermen are allowed to catch and when, with the by product of any catch seen as 'discard'. Instead of being able to take this discard to market, fishermen are ordered to throw it back to the sea - dead. The punishment for those 'over-fishing' can be legal proceedings at the hands of the EU, with substantial fines being imposed. Thankfully the Common Fisheries Policy is set to change, with conservation science effectively setting catch limits, previously subject to political negotiations. Here are the thoughts of some of our restaurateurs on the quota fiasco.

THE situation with the by-product from fishing quotas is one of the biggest crimes of the last 100 years. There's no clever management of it and what we need is to manage our stocks properly," Graham Suttle, Finnieston and Lebowski's.

SANDRO at La Parmigiana: "What saddens me about the fish is that fishermen get a net full of fish, and if it's not what they are supposed to catch, they have to throw it back dead. It's a complete waste. If you go to Italy, France or Spain they have the same restrictions – but restaurants there are using the by-product. Europe is great with putting stupid rules into place, but those countries never adhere to them, yet we do."

ANDY at Rogano: "If you put out a net and look for cod and pull something out other than that, you're supposed to put them back. But what's the point in that - it's a complete waste to me. There are just so many restrictions on what fishermen are allowed to catch and what we can buy, but half of it's nonsense. I use the analogy that it's like giving my wife £1000 and sending her to Buchanan Street to spend it, but telling her she only has five minutes to do so. She's going to buy everything and anything, and inevitably it's going to be the wrong stuff or stuff she doesn't need."

Wine Pairing:
This dish combines
the taste of the sea with more
earthy peas and pork. To match that
complex blend of flavors, a rich and
dry white wine like a Condrieu (France),
with its minerality and bursting flavors of
flowers and ripe yellow fruits, would make
the perfect partner. For red wine lovers,
a Pinot Noir from Central Otago (New
Zealand), which is light and fresh, but
with a subtle hint of spices to add
more contrast, would be a great
alternative.

This dish is served
in Turnberry's award-
winning James Miller Room
and is a memorable dish
prepared using local Scottish
produce. The Turnberry Chefs
also forage in the grounds of
the resort for fresh garnishes,
such as wild garlic.

Maidens Road, Turnberry
Ayrshire KA26 9LT
T: 01655 331 000

Halibut, Peas, and Pork Jowl

For the Pork Jowl:
- 1 Whole pork jowl
- 4 Cups plus 2 tbsp Veal stock
- 1 Bay leaf
- 4 Sprigs thyme
- 1 Bulb garlic, cloves peeled and crushed

For the Shallot Confit:
- 5 Whole shallots
- 1 Cup olive oil

For the Halibut:
- ½ lb North Sea halibut
- 1/3oz Serrano ham, julienned
- 0.2oz Fresh black truffles, sliced
- 0.2oz Wild garlic, whole

For the Pea Purée:
- ¾ Cup chicken stock
- 7oz Fresh peas, shelled
- 2 tbsp Unsalted butter
- Salt to taste

For the Pea Velouté:
- 5 Large shallots
- 1.8oz Wild seasonal mushrooms
- 1 tbsp Unsalted butter
- 3.5oz Sea scallops
- 1 Bay leaf
- ½ Bulb garlic
- 1 Sprig thyme
- 3 tbsp Plus a teaspoon of white wine
- 3 tbsp Plus a teaspoon of double cream

- 10.5oz Fresh peas in shells
- Salt to taste
- Juice of ½ a lemon

For the Fresh Peas:
- ¾ oz Wild garlic leaves
- ¾ tsp Garlic purée
- 4 tbsp Unsalted butter, softened
- ¼ Cup plus three tablespoons chicken stock
- 1.75oz Fresh peas in shells

For the Pea Foam:
- ¾ Cup plus one tablespoon pea velouté (above)
- ¾ Cup plus one tablespoon chicken stock
- 0.03oz Lecithin

99

Preheat the oven to 325°F
Start by cooking the pork jowl. Put a large sauté pan over high heat. When the pan is very hot, sear the pork jowl until golden brown on both sides. Add the veal stock, bay leaf, thyme, and garlic. Put all ingredients into a roasting pan, cover, and cook for about 90mins in the oven.
Make the shallots confit. Put the unpeeled shallots in a pot over low heat and cover with the oil. Cook until soft. Take them out of the oil and let them cool. Peel the shallots and set aside.
Prepare the halibut. Remove the skin and bones from the fish. Cut out the center piece of meat for use, making sure there is no brown meat. Make six small incisions in the fish and stuff with ham, truffles, and wild garlic.
Make the pea purée. Bring the chicken stock to rapid boil and add the fresh peas. Cook just until soft, but still bright green. Drain and put in a high-speed blender, adding butter gradually and a little stock to achieve a smooth consistency. Cool very quickly over ice to maintain color. Season to taste.
Make the pea velouté. Place the shallots and mushrooms in a sauté pan over medium-low heat with a little butter and sweat just until soft – do not let them brown. Add the scallops, bay leaf, garlic, and thyme. Then add the white wine, simmering til reduced by half. Add the cream, bring to a boil, and remove from heat. Shell the peas and add shells

to the cream, cover, and allow to cool. Strain the mixture, put the liquid in a high-speed blender and add the fresh peas. Strain again to get rid of any pea shells, and season with salt and lemon juice.
Prepare the fresh peas. Bring a pot of water to a boil. Add the wild garlic leaves and blanch just until tender and vibrant green; plunge into ice water to refresh; drain. Add the wild garlic and garlic purée to the butter and blend until smooth; pass through a fine sieve and cover with plastic wrap. Bring the chicken stock to a boil and add the garlic butter. Shell the peas and add them to the butter stock, cooking just until the peas are soft.
Make the pea foam. Take a little of the pea velouté and add a little chicken stock to loosen. Add the lecithin and use a hand-held blender to make a foam.
Cook the halibut. Place a non-stick pan over medium heat. Sear the halibut skin side up. Flip the fish and sear other side. Add a little butter to the pan and place in the oven, baking til cooked through – about 8-12 minutes.
To serve. Heat the pork jowl in a little reduced veal stock until sticky. Smear some pea purée on each plate and place a serving of halibut next to it. Build the garnish on top of the pea purée, starting with the pork jowl, then the shallots confit, then the fresh peas, then a little pool of velouté. Finish with the pea foam.

Vito's restaurant in Ayr is run by Stephen Conetta who knows the importance of using locally sourced produce, freshly cooked to order. Vito's is ideal for a romantic dinner for two or an evening with friends and family. He tells us how the food scene has changed in Ayrshire in recent years.

HE said: "Things have definitely improved in the food scene and it is great at the moment. Glasgow and Ayrshire have got some great stuff going on and I think it's fantastic.

"People are starting to become more knowledgeable about food and are willing to try more. The good thing about Ayrshire is the independent opportunities. In the restaurant, you get to listen to customers and talk to them, and see what they like, what keeps them happy - so we run specials that change and we try to get something different for the customers that they don't have. It's good to give them the chance to come back as regulars.

"The food scene in Ayrshire is definitely on the up and the footfall in the restaurant is definitely greater than it was last year. There's more restaurants than last year too, and the ones that were here, are all still here."

Fresh Mushroom Ravioli

25 Burns Statue Square
Ayr KA7 1SU
T: 01292 290 777

For the pasta:
• 275g Strong oo flour
• 2 Large free range eggs

For the filling:
• 50g Diced white onion
• 100g Sliced mushrooms

• 3 Large free range egg yolks
• 1 tbsp Olive oil
• Pinch salt
• 1 tsp Freshly cut flat leaf parsley
• 1 tsp Chopped garlic
• 20ml Dry white wine

Sieve flour and place in food processor. Add eggs, oil and salt. Mix into breadcrumbs – add a few drops of cold water to achieve this consistency if needed.

Remove from processor and place on lightly floured surface. Knead until dough is smooth. Wrap in clingfilm and place in fridge for at least an hour. Meanwhile, in a heavy bottomed pot, saute onion in a little oil with a touch of seasoning. Add the parsley, garlic and lightly fry after a few minutes. Once onion is cooked, add mushrooms and gently cook. Add wine and reduce cooking liquid until almost completely evaporated. Remove from heat and use electric hand blender till almost smooth. Check seasoning and adjust as necessary – set aside to cool.

Remove pasta from fridge, taking a piece about the size of a small orange – seal remaining dough and place back in fridge.

Using a rolling pin, flatten dough until roughly the thickness of a one pound coin. Set pasta machine to thickest setting and feed the dough through. Keep adjusting the setting by one until you have reached the thinnest setting, where upon the dough will be almost transparent.

Place two sheets of pasta parallel to each other on a lightly floured surface. Using your mushroom filling, place one tablespoon of the mixture at regular intervals along the dough.

Now place remaining sheet on top and, using forefingers, seal around the mixture knocking any air out. Cut your ravioli shapes trying to make each one identical. For maximum effect, serve three or four large ravioli, rather than many small ones. Press down with a fork around the ravioli shape to seal mixture inside and create a presentable shape. Heat a pot of salted water until boiling and drop in pasta. Cook for no more than 2-3mins. Remove from water and serve in a light mushroom and cream sauce.

Garnish with freshly blitzed basil oil, parmesan shavings and fresh rocket.

IF you think golf and Ayrshire, the first place that will spring to mind is Turnberry. And if you think Turnberry, the first thing that will spring to mind is five star.

And that's exactly what you'll get from dining at the resort's 1906 restaurant. With one of the most picturesque views you'll find on Scotland's stunning West Coast, the panoramic vista over the Irish Sea perfectly frames Ailsa Craig and Arran.

But it's not just the view and five star surroundings that will leave diners awestruck, with first class fayre served up in abundance too.

It's a tantalising culinary journey inspired by the land, river and sea that surroundings the resort, with Head Chef, Munur Kara presenting classical French Escoffier dishes with a modern twist, including the most tender steaks and freshest seafood, all of which are created using the finest local ingredients.

Definitely at the high end of the dining spectrum, there is great value to be found, as diners can enjoy an outstanding Sunday Brunch offer on the first Sunday of every month from 12.30pm – 3pm.

Turnberry offers up some of the best food Scotland has to offer and is a must visit.

IDEALLY placed in Ayr's historic town centre, Vito's contemporary restaurant is just a few hundred yards from Ayr train station and the epicentre of the town's night life.

A relaxed atmosphere, excellent views over the historic Burns Statue Square can be enjoyed by over 100 people over two floors, linked by a stunning glass staircase. Vito's is ideal for a romantic dinner for two, an evening with friends, and even dinner parties and celebrations.

Serving up authentic stone baked pizzas, a range of pastas, chargrilled steaks and burgers, seafood and homemade desserts, Vito's showcases fantastic Italian dishes using the best of Scotland's larder.

That includes traditional veal dishes, which Head Chef and proprietor, Stephen Conetta is proud to place on a menu full of great quality dishes that provide great value for money.

Friendly, knowledgeable staff talk diners through dishes and menus with ease, with a variety of specials also on offer.

Traditional pizza, pasta, and homemade Italian desserts in the heart of Burns' country – what more could you ask for?

BETTER known for its fine cheddar and cheese, Dunlop is also host to one of Ayrshire's best kept secrets – Struther Farmhouse.

The beautiful traditional farmhouse is a real treasure trove and has been one of the best kept secrets for four decades.

With two restaurants for diners to choose from, large and medium sized parties can be accommodated, but couples and small groups will benefit from the distinctive ambience, privacy and intimacy each room has to offer.

Striving to cater for all, Struther's has a fine offering for vegans with all offerings of food made from fresh local produce.

And not being licensed, it is one of the few restaurants these days operating a 'bring your own drinks' policy, with no corkage charge.

Gorgeous homemade, traditional meals can be snapped up for incredible value, with deals serving up four course dinners, with coffee and petit fours for less than £30. They even provide buffet meals to enjoy in your own home.

Local, knowledgeable and professional staff, provide relaxed service befitting of the surroundings.

ARRAN is a fine destination serving up some of Scotland's best produce. Whether the beer, whisky, cheese or wine, its 'exports' are a fine addition to Scotland's larder.

And the island is more than capable of serving up something special for those on the island, be it residents or visitors. One such place is Café Thyme owned by Hamza Gunaydi and Lorna Mansfield.

With Turkish and Scottish backgrounds, the menu serves up the best of both cuisines, making the most of a specially built wood-burning oven for Chef Gunaydi's signature breads and pides.

Pides, a flatbread pizza, offers something truly different for diners, with the haggis version a fine example of the two cultures marrying.

A keenly priced menu serves up traditional Turkish favourites, including lamb kofte kebab and baklava. The flip side of the coin sees Scottish favourites too, with oatmeal-coated mackerel showcasing the talents of the chef and the produce available.

Traditional dishes, such as fish and chips, are offset by modern treats, such as wild boar and apple burger.

Machrie may be a place overlooked by most visitors to Arran, but with fine eateries like this, it could soon find itself swarming with hungry travellers.

104 Leek, bacon and goats cheese tarts

Newmill Road
Dunlop
Kilmarnock KA3 4BA
T: 01560 484946

This is a real customer favourite dish and we have used it for many years as a starter on our Christmas menu. It uses a lot of local ingredients and is very popular with guests.

- 4 Sheets of filo pastry
- 1 Large leek
- 1 Onion
- 50g Butter
- 80g Ayrshire bacon
- 15g Plain flour
- 30ml Cream
- 80g Soft rind Clerkland Farm (Dunlop) goats cheese

To start, melt the butter and brush each filo sheet with a little. Then, fold the pastry into 10cm squares - there should be enough pastry to fit four greased Yorkshire pudding tins.

Lightly brush the top of the tartlets with butter and bake at gas 180°C or gas mark 4 until light brown in colour.

Whilst tartlets are cooking, add the chopped onion and chopped bacon to the remaining butter and gently cook until onions are translucent. Now add the finely chopped leek, cooking until soft.

Stir in the flour and cream, seasoning the mix with sea salt and ground pepper to taste.

When ready, split the leek mixture between the four tarts and top with a slice of goats cheese. Place the Yorkshire tins with tarts into the oven to warm for 15mins at 140°C.

Serve with salad as a starter or light lunch.

A nice side:

A great side dish to serve with fish and meat dishes is just plain carrots. Done well, these can be a real treat. They're nice and simple, but to get the best flavour you need to buy quality, dirty carrots.

Wash, peel, top and tail the carrots, keeping whole. Add salt to water and place the carrots in – bring slowly to the boil and simmer until a sharp knife can easily be cut through the carrots.

To serve, just add a little butter. To dress them up, add some parsley and crushed fennel seeds.

Top tip:

Potatoes for roasting - Golden Wonder
Potatoes for mashing - Maris Piper
Potatoes for boiling - Charlotte

Pides

Machrie
Isle of Arran KA27 8EB
T: 01770 840608

Pides are Café Thyme's speciality and, like all food here, lovingly produced from the wood burning oven. We describe them as a Turkish style pizza, however they're like a calzone, but it's difficult to do them justice without trying them. There are many fillings from crayfish, artichoke, smoked venison, chicken, spinach and haggis and cheese. Below are just a couple of suggestions:

Pide dough:
• 480g Plain flour.
• 375ml Warm water
• 1 tbsp Yeast

• Pinch sugar
• 1 tsp Salt
• Mix dough and leave overnight in the fridge to rise

Filling for steak mince and sun dried tomato option:
Cooked steak mince with onion, oregano, sun dried tomato, salt and black pepper.
Take 160g of dough and shape into a boat, fill with mince and fold to seal at top.
Bake in the wood burning oven at 240°C for approximately 10mins
Remove and brush with melted butter, slice and serve straight away

Filling for Chicken pide:
Cooked chicken, fry with tomato, pepper, spring onion, garlic, thyme, salt and black pepper.
Take 160g dough and shape into a boat, bake in oven for three minutes keeping the boat shape
Remove and fill chicken mixture inside boat and bake at 240°C for approximately five minutes.
Remove and sprinkle with mozzarella and bake for another 2-3mins.
Remove and brush edges with melted butter – serve immediately.

Bloggers

Former university lecturer, Briony Cullin tells us how blogging helped her start a new career and talks about the importance of bloggers to the food scene in Glasgow.

THE Yelp Community Manager for Glasgow said: "I think recently there has been a number of places opening up almost weekly and it's exciting to see that. There's obviously a huge demand for it from people in Glasgow. They're wanting to try new things and new tastes, and now businesses are seeing that and looking to take advantage. If one place opens up, then it can start a trend – just look at the Bubble Tea in the Savoy Centre. It opened up first and now there are a few similar places throughout the city.

"I think Glasgow is one of the best places to be for food lovers. You can usually find something a little different or something you've wanted to try for a while. It's got a great mix of places. It's never going to be a London or New York, the type of cities that start worldwide trends, but its got so much variety. For the amount of places I eat at through my work, there are still about 100 places I'm dying to try out.

"I moved to Glasgow from Melbourne, which is a city where people are almost reliant on bloggers to get the feel for where to go. Bloggers are very important in Melbourne culture, so when I came here I looked to bloggers to find my feet in terms of places I wanted to go, but there weren't that many. I started blogging to show my friends back home that Glasgow was a good place to be for food and as a hobby in a new place. I never thought it would become my career. I've only been in Glasgow for four years, but it's already my home.

"I think James vs. Burger is the best example of the importance of blogging. He has been very influential for the food scene in Glasgow. He's responsible for the number of burger joints that Glasgow now has and he has done the blog really well, giving an insight into that almost American culture of a burger and shake.

"To be successful, I think restaurants are going to want to have access to all kinds of social media.

It's very rare for a business not to have an online presence these days. Some of the biggest opening in 2013 were created via blogging and Twitter, which helped to create the buzz surrounding the ventures. Places like the Meat Bar, Burger Meats Bun, and the Gannet were on the tip of everyone's tongue before they had even opened, such was the online hype.

"This is a really big time for Glasgow. That positive energy is going to bring a huge amount of opportunity and variety to the city. It will bring new and different experiences to the food scene here, experiences that are fresh, healthy, packed full of flavour – not just a greasy sausage roll from the bakers. There are so many different cultures and flavours in the food scene at the moment, and that is going to see that increase massively. That will see an increase in the amount of bloggers – people love talking about this stuff and feeling as if they have an influence. And they do."

Beef Stew

For Beef stew
- 1kg beef brisket, cut into nine bar chunks
- Dusting flour
- Vegetable oil
- 200g Smoked bacon cubes
- 1 large onion
- 4 carrots
- 10 Cherry tomatoes
- Sprig of thyme
- 1tsp Herb de Provence
- 500ml Red wine
- 100ml Water
- 1 Tbsp Tomato puree
- 10 Button mushrooms

For Mash Potato
- 3 Medium size potatoes (Maris Piper or Desiree)
- 60g butter
- Salt and Pepper

Methodology

Step 1.
Cut beef brisket and coat with flour and salt. Heat oil and pan fry till browned, but not charred

Step 2.
Retain oil and stir fry finely chopped up onion and one carrot

Step 3.
Return beef to pot. Add 500ml wine and 100ml water, tomato purée, thyme and herbs. Boil till alcohol evaporates and reduce heat to low and simmer for two hours until beef is tender

Step 4.
Add largely chopped carrots, mushrooms and tomatoes in the last 15mins of cooking

Step 5.
For the mash, peel and boil largely chopped potatoes for 20mins. Drain water, add butter and mash. Season with salt and pepper.

Michelle Muirhead
@ananyah
ananyah.com

Machboos Laham - Lamb And Rice With Daqoos

For the Meat & Rice
- 3 kg Scottish lamb shanks
- 4 cups basmati rice
- 6 cups water
- 2 tbsp finely chopped onion
- 2 tbsp ghee or vegetable oil
- 2 sticks cinnamon
- 8 cardamom pods
- 8 cloves
- 1 bay leaf
- ½ tsp turmeric powder
- 1 tbsp saffron strands
- ¼ cup rose water
- 1 tsp ground cardamom
- 2 tbsp salt

For the Hashoo (Onion Garnish)
- 1 large onion chopped
- ½ cup golden raisins
- 1 tbsp garam masala
- 1 tbsp ghee or vegetable oil
- 1 tsp salt

For the Daqoos (Tomato Sauce)
- 5 tomatoes chopped
- 5 cloves garlic minced
- 2 tbsp tomato paste
- 2 tbsp vegetable oil
- ½ tsp salt
- ½ tsp paprika

Methodology

Step 1. Soak rice in water, wash gently and drain to dry. Wash lamb shank carefully and rub with turmeric powder and a bit of salt. Marinate for 30mins, then wash again.

Step 2. Heat oil in deep pot. Fry onion, cinnamon sticks, cardamom, cloves, and bay leaf quickly, then add lamb. Stir until browned completely and cover for 10mins. Add six cups boiling water, bring to a boil. Lower heat and leave to simmer for two hours.

Step 3. Make sure the water doesn't dry out. It's okay if the water doesn't cover the meat, it will still cook the meat while occasionally stirring. When done, remove lamb from the broth. In a small cup add heated rose water, saffron and cardamom powder.

Step 4. Meanwhile fry the hashoo mix in a pan over a low heat until the onions become deep brown and set aside.

Step 5. For the daqoos, in a small sauce pan heat oil and quickly fry garlic and mix in the tomatoes. Simmer and cover for 10mins. Mix in tomato paste, paprika and salt and simmer for a further 10 minutes. If you'd like a thinner consistency, add more water to dilute it down.

Step 6. In another deep pot, heat oil and add the washed and soaked basmati rice. Fry for three minutes until oil is fully soaked into the rice. Pour the lamb broth on the rice. Make sure the broth is approximately an inch above the rice level.

Step 7. Add 2 tbsp oil and 1½ tbsp salt. Stir gently once, bring to a boil, cover and simmer over low heat for 15-20mins, ensuring it doesn't burn.

Step 8. Fry lamb again with vegetable oil and garam masala for three minutes.

Step 9. When the rice is done, pour the rose water and saffron mixture into the rice, add the lamb shanks on top with the hashoo on the side. Cover and let it rest on very low heat for around 30mins to allow the flavours to develop.

Step 10. Serve rice, lamb and hashoo together with some daqoos on the side.

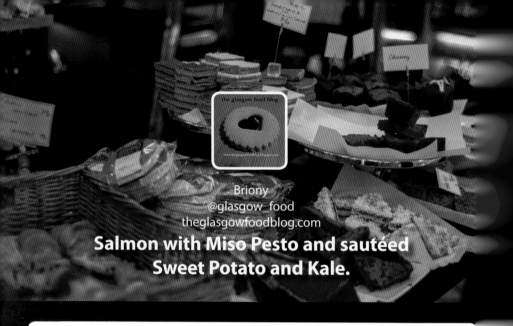

Briony
@glasgow_food
theglasgowfoodblog.com

Salmon with Miso Pesto and sautéed Sweet Potato and Kale.

- 2 Scottish salmon fillets
- 4 tbsp panko breadcrumbs
- 1 tbsp coconut oil or butter
- 1 large sweet potato, peeled and diced
- 100g kale, stalks removed
- 4 tbsp soy sauce/tamari

Miso pesto
- 1 tbsp miso paste
- 1 cup of spinach
- 1 cup of coriander
- ½ cup pitted green olives
- 50g almonds
- ¼ cup olive oil
- Juice of one lemon

Methodology

Step 1.
Pre heat oven to 180C.

Step 2.
Make miso pesto by adding all ingredients to a blender and blending until thoroughly combined.

Step 3.
Line a baking sheet with baking paper. Place salmon fillets on the sheet, spreading with miso paste – around a tablespoon per fillet. Cook in oven for 10mins. Remove, adding panko breadcrumbs to the layer of pesto. Bake for a further four minutes, then remove and keep warm.

Step 4.
In a large frying pan on medium heat, add coconut oil. Once heated, add in diced sweet potato and cook for around six minutes or until sweet potato is tender.

Step 5.
Add kale to sweet potato and stir through. Allow around four minutes for kale to sauté and reduce. Dress the kale and sweet potato with soy sauce to taste.

Step 6.
Serve the sweet potato and kale topped with a salmon fillet.

Divya
@the_fussy_eater
Providing recipes for Fussy Eaters like me
fussyeater.net

Asian Inspired Langoustines

- 10 Langoustines, heads removed and cut in half lengthways
- 1 tsp ginger and garlic paste
- 1 tsp lemongrass paste
- 1 tsp Shaoxing wine
- 2 tsp light soy sauce
- 1 tsp oyster sauce
- ½ tsp fish sauce
- ½ tsp sesame oil
- 1 ½ tsp water
- 1 bunch spring onions, sliced
- 1 red chilli, sliced
- 3 Kaffir lime leaves (optional)

Methodology

Step 1.
Put everything except langoustines, lime leaves, spring onions and chilli in a bowl and mix.

Step 2.
Now add langoustines and mix well.

Step 3.
Place lime leaves with ½ the spring onions and chillies in bottom of a pan.

Step 4.
Arrange langoustines over this and pour over any excess marinade.

Step 5.
Scatter remaining spring onions and chillies over the langoustines.

Step 6.
Turn heat up to high and cook for 5 – 7mins.

Step 7.
Serve immediately with freshly boiled rice and stir fried vegetables.

Sweet Chilli Pork and Chorizo Burgers
This recipe is great for warm summer days, when we're lucky enough to get them in Glasgow. The pork is slightly lighter than beef, and the sweet chilli sauce, chorizo and red onion really lift the flavour. Enjoy this one outside, with an ice cold bottle of wheat beer.

400g of pork mince
Salt
Pepper
100g chorizo sausage, finely diced (skin removed)
3 tbsp sweet chilli sauce

1 tsp dried coriander
3 tbsp breadcrumbs
1 onion, grated
1 red onion, finely sliced
1 beef tomato, sliced

1 egg
Applewood cheese, sliced (as much as you like)
Lettuce
Burger buns
(Makes 4 burgers)

The buns:
Slice each bun in half and place face down on a dry frying pan over a medium heat until lightly toasted. These will toast quickly. Remove and set aside

The patties:
Mix together the pork mince, chorizo, white onion, garlic, sweet chilli sauce, coriander, breadcrumbs and egg with your hands. Season with salt and pepper, then shape and form into four patties. Once prepared, fry the burgers in some oil over a medium heat for roughly 5-6 mins (or until done) on each side.

Build the burgers:
Layer the burgers as follows: bottom half of bun, lettuce, patty, Applewood cheese, tomato, red onion, top half of bun. Spread a little more sweet chilli sauce on the top half of the bun before you place it on.
Once you've done this, lightly wrap the burgers in tin foil and place them on the bottom shelf of the oven for around five minutes. This will heat the entire burger a little more and further melt the cheese, meat, sauce and toppings all together for a great look and finish.

Peanut Butter Cheeseburgers

I know what you're thinking, 'why would you ever want to put peanut butter on a burger?' The answer, simply, is because it's incredible. I first discovered these during a trip to New York a few years ago and since then they've become a huge hit in our house. Peanut butter isn't just for spreading on your toast, it works well in quite a lot of other dishes. So don't be scared; try these burgers, even if you think they sound disgusting. After your first bite, you'll be glad you did.

INGREDIENTS:

250g beef mince
1 tbsp wholegrain mustard
4 slices American Cheese
2 heaped tablespoons of smooth peanut butter
Tomato ketchup
American mustard

Bun – a brioche burger bun works well, but any kind will do
2 egg yolks
1/2 cup breadcrumbs
Salt and pepper
Makes two burgers

Again, pre-heat your oven, then prepare the buns as before. Leave the bottom half of each bun dry and on the top half of each, apply a generous helping of tomato ketchup and American mustard. Set aside.

In a large bowl combine the mince, wholegrain mustard, a pinch of salt, a dash of pepper, the egg yolks and breadcrumbs. Mix everything together and roll mince into two golf ball-sized shapes. Heat up a skillet or pan with a little oil.

Sprinkle a little salt on the one side of the meat only. Place the ball of meat into the hot pan (salt side down). Cook for one minute. Sprinkle salt on the top and flip over. At this point you want to 'smash' the patty down.

To 'smash' it, simply press down on the patty with a fish slice until it reaches your desired look. Flip and cook until done and the juices run clear. Add the American cheese to the top of the patties (two on each one) while they are still in the pan. Once they start to melt a little, remove from heat.

Place the patties on the bottom half of each bun, add a generous heaped tablespoon of smooth peanut butter to each and gently spread across each patty. Add the top half of the bun.

Almost done. Again, wrap the finished burger lightly in tin foil and place in the oven for a few minutes. For an even more indulgent experience, you can also try adding a couple of slices of crispy bacon to your burger.

VS.

THE ULTIMATE BURGER JOURNEY

Gerry's Kitchen
@Gerrys_Kitchen
Recipes, Reviews & Ramblings of a hungry man
Glasgow · gerryskitchen.blogspot.com

Chicken Katsu Curry

- 2 chicken breasts
- Seasoned flour
- 1 egg, beaten
- 100g panko breadcrumbs
- 1 onion, finely diced
- 2 garlic cloves, chopped
- Small piece of ginger, finely chopped

- Pinch of chilli flakes
- 1 tbsp plain flour
- 1 tbsp curry powder
- 350 ml chicken stock
- 100g basmati rice
- Sesame oil
- Dark soy sauce

Methodology

Step 1.
Dip chicken breasts in seasoned flour, then the beaten egg, before covering all over with panko breadcrumbs. Refrigerate for 10mins before cooking.

Step 2.
Heat some oil in a frying pan and cook chicken breasts for 2 – 3mins each side before transferring to baking tray – place in a pre-heated oven at 180ºC for 20mins.

Step 3.
For the curry sauce, put onion, garlic, ginger & chilli flakes in a saucepan with a little olive oil. Cook for about 5mins. Add flour and curry powder, stirring at the start to stop contents catching on the bottom. Add chicken stock and bring to the boil, stirring continuously.

Step 4.
Reduce the heat and continue to cook for 15mins. Blend sauce to a smooth consistency. Remove the sauce from heat and set aside.

Step 5.
Cook the rice in plenty of salted water before adding peas for last couple of minutes cooking. Drain before stirring through a splash of sesame oil and dark soy sauce.

Food Drink Glasgow
@GlasgowFoodie
foodanddrinkglasgow.co.uk

Plokkfiskur

- 560g cooked haddock or cod
- 560g boiled and peeled potatoes
- 1 white onion finely chopped
- 350ml milk
- 55g butter

- 3 tbsp flour
- Salt and pepper
- 2 tbsp chives
- Rye bread

Methodology

Step 1.
Skin, bone and break up fish into flakes

Step 2.
Roughly chop potatoes

Step 3.
Slowly heat milk in a saucepan almost to a boiling point. In a separate pan, over a medium heat, melt butter and saute onion until soft, but do not brown.

Step 4.
Sprinkle flour over onion, stir well and cook for 1-2mins. Gradually add warmed milk, stirring continuously. Simmer for 3-4mins, stirring.

Step 5.
Add flaked fish and stir briskly to break up fish completely. Season liberally with salt and pepper.

Step 6.
Add potatoes and stir gently. Cook over low-heat till heated through.

Step 7.
Spoon onto rye bread and sprinkle with chives. Can also be decorated with eggs.

Girl Around Glasgow
@girlaroundglasg
Glasgow, UK · girlaroundglasgow.wordpress.com

Pork medallions in an Apple and Mustard sauce with Chickpea and Butternut squash mash

- 6 to 8 slices of pork medallions OR pork loin cut into 1½ in pieces
- 400 g tin of chickpeas, drained and washed
- 2/3 of a butternut squash, peeled and diced into 1 cm

- 3 tbsp olive oil plus 1 tbsp for the pork
- 150 ml good quality medium dry cider
- 1 large apple
- 3 tbsp hot water
- 2 heaped tsp dijon mustard

- 2 tbsp single cream OR crème fraiche
- 3 tbsp snipped chives
- 150g green beans
- Salt and pepper

Methodology

Step 1. Preheat oven to 200ºC/fan 180ºC

Step 2. Put chickpeas and butternut squash onto large baking tray and sprinkle with salt and pepper. Use your hands to coat well. Cook in the middle of the preheated oven for 20mins, tossing regularly to ensure even cooking

Step 3. Season pork and leave to rest at room temp

Step 4. Peel and core the apple, slicing it lengthways into 12 pieces and submerging in cold water to prevent discolouring

Step 5. Bring a frying pan to a medium heat, adding one tablespoon of oil. Add pork and cook for about three minutes each side. Remove pork and place into a pouch made of tin foil. Wrap tightly to keep warm

Step 6. Now add apple slices and hot water to the pan juices, softening the fruit, turning every so often until the water has been soaked up. Add cider and mustard to the pan and season. Reduce mixture by half, making sure apples are soft

Step 7. Boil a pan full of water and add the beans – cook for about four minutes, then drain

Step 8. Meanwhile, once cider mixture has reduced, turn the heat down to low and add cream and two tablespoons of chives. Open the foil pork package and pour any pork juice into the sauce then re-close the package – stir and taste then add the pork

Step 9. Take the chickpea and squash mixture out the oven after 20mins and transfer into a big bowl or pan, then mash

Step 10. Put your mash on to plates and top with the pork and sauce. Serve with green beans and season with chives

Glasgow Food Geek
@Glasgowfoodgeek
glasgowfoodgeek.co.uk

Bolognese a la Food Geek

- 2 Glugs of olive oil
- 100g Bacon Lardons
- 3tsp dried oregano
- 2 Medium onions
- 2 Garlic cloves

- 3 Medium carrots
- 3 Medium sticks of celery
- 500g Mince - either lean beef or pork
- 2 x 400g Tins of tomatoes

- Fresh basil
- 150g Parmesan Cheese
- Your favourite, good quality pasta

Methodology

Step 1. Dice onion, garlic, carrots and celery.

Step 2. Place a large pot over a high/medium heat, add olive oil and allow pan to heat up for a few minutes. Throw in diced bacon lardons and dried oregano. Fry until bacon turns a lovely golden colour; this normally takes a couple of minutes.

Step 3. Next, add diced onion, garlic, carrots and celery to pot stirring regularly for 6-8mins until veg softens slightly.

Step 4. Add mince and tomatoes to pot - fill both tomato tins with cold water and stir into the mixture. Grab a few basil stems, chop and throw into the pot (put basil leaves into fridge for now, as you'll need them later). Add salt and pepper to sauce, mix and bring to boil.

Step 5. Once boiling, reduce heat and cover pan with lid. The sauce will need approx one hour to simmer, stir about every 20 minutes to prevent sticking.

Step 6. Once sauce has simmered remove it from heat - add approx 100g of grated Parmesan and rip basil leaves into halves, adding to sauce. Mix this through and your sauce is ready

Step 7. Cook pasta following instructions, drain pasta and place pasta back into pan. Add some sauce to pasta and mix together well. Serve pasta up onto plates, grate some of the remaining 50g of Parmesan over the top of the pasta and it's ready to eat.

Step 8. If you are freezing the bolognese sauce ensure it is completely cooled before freezing.

Stovies Samosas

- 1 Onion, cut into centimetre chunks
- 1 Carrot, cut into centimetre chunks
- 10 Green beans, cut into centimetre chunks or 100g petit pois
- 2 – 3 Medium potatoes, cut into centimetre chunks
- 2 Garlic cloves

- 1 Stalk of rosemary
- 1in Piece of root ginger
- 250g Minced beef
- 1 Beef stock cube
- 250ml Boiling water
- Oil for frying
- 20 Samosa wrappers - alternatively 10 spring roll wrappers or 10 tortilla wraps

- 1tsp Cumin seeds
- 1tsp Coriander seeds or ground coriander
- 1 Chilli, de-seeded
- 1tsp Garam masala
- Salt & pepper
- 1tsp Cornflour, mixed with
- 3tbsp Water

Methodology

Step 1 Add carrot, onion, green beans and potatoes to a pot with one tablespoon of oil. Cook, covered, over a medium heat for 10mins until softened. Add the mince and chopped rosemary. Increase heat to medium/high, browning mince

Step 2 Toast whole spices in dry pan over medium heat up to a minute. Grind into fine powder using pestle and mortar. Once browned, add spices to mince with teaspoon of water. Grate in ginger and garlic. Season with salt and pepper, crumbling in stock cube.

Step 3 Pour boiling water over mince and bring to rapid boil. Reduce to rapid simmer, cook partially covered for 30 – 40mins, stirring regularly. Mixture should now have thickened. Decant into bowl, leaving to cool – if possible, overnight. This is your Stovie mix

Step 4 Cooking: you can use deep fat fryer, or heat inch of oil in heavy based frying pan, pot or wok. In a small cup, mix cornflour and water to form milky water. Set aside until ready to seal samosas

Step 5 If using samosa wrappers, use two for every parcel as very thin. If spring roll wrappers, cut into strips approx three inches wide. Do the same with tortilla wraps but discard strips with rounded edges.

Step 6 Lay a strip in front of you and spoon on a good teaspoon of filling at top edge. Fold top left corner down to meet right edge, forming a triangle. Fold triangle pocket towards you, then fold again towards left side of pastry. Fold once more towards yourself until you reach edge of pastry strip and filling is encased inside triangle of pastry

Step 7 Use fingertips to brush some of milky water around overhang of the pastry. Fold over samosa, pressing down to seal. Set aside on a chopping board while wrapping the rest.

Step 8 Use a kitchen thermometer to test oil temperature. You want 175 – 190C. Alternatively, toss a small chunk of bread into oil – if it turns crispy within a minute, the oil is ready. Fry samosas in batches until golden. This will take up to two minutes each side. Drain on some kitchen roll, before serving piled onto a plate with sweet Thai chilli sauce for dipping and ice cold beers.

TRISTAN Hugh-Jones of the Lochryan Oyster Company talks about the food scene in Scotland, highlighting some of the key issues.

He tells us: "The provenance of food is a massive selling point for restaurants and the ones that use us love showcasing that provenance and the quality of the oysters. The story of how they are caught and when can be followed, identifying the actual fisherman that caught the oysters – that can all be traced and it is a massive selling point for us and restaurants.

"The sustainability and ethical way in which produce is prepared is massively important to the consumer these days. And that's the future for our food scene – to be more open and proud of that. The average customer now wants to know more about where their food comes from and they care about that. We can't look away from that and you can't ignore it. I think everyone is aware of caring for the sea environment, they know the reasons the quotas are in place and they know when they are catching too much – but the by-product regulations are unfair.

"I think there's much more interest in provenance of food in general. Previously you would go to a restaurant and see plain old oysters on the menu. Now you go to restaurants and there are a number of different types of oysters, showcasing the provenance and merits of each kind.

"For someone's first oyster, I would always say just try it as it is. Second time round with a squeeze of lemon, third time with Tabasco, and then with an onion dressing. Rock oysters are better oysters to cook with as they are meatier, maybe just under the grill with a few bits and breadcrumbs on top."

mary's meals

a simple solution to world hunger

Magnus with some of the children Mary's Meals has helped in Haiti

MARY'S Meals is a global movement that sets up school feeding projects in some of the world's poorest communities, where poverty and hunger prevent children from gaining an education.

What began in 2002 as a simple famine relief programme has become an international charity, now feeding over 820,000 children every school day in 16 countries. The commitment of the charity to keep running costs as low as possible ensures 93% of all donations are spent on charitable work.

And with the average worldwide cost to feed a child for the whole school year being £10.70 (just six pence per meal), the small contribution made by purchasing the 'Foodies' Guide to Glasgow and the West' will go a long way to help chronically hungry children, giving them a hope for the future.

Mary's Meals Chief Executive and founder, Magnus MacFarlane-Barrow told us: "Today, around the world, 57 million children miss school because of poverty. Instead of sitting in a classroom gaining an education, they are working in fields, begging on street corners, or scavenging among the garbage to survive.

"Millions more attend school so hungry they are not able to concentrate and learn. Our vision is that every hungry child should be able to receive one good meal each day they attend school and in this world of plenty there is no reason why that can't happen. Over three quarters of a million of the world's poorest children now receive Mary's Meals every day in their place of education, but there are many more who need our help. We currently have lists of schools waiting to be added to our feeding programme in communities where local volunteers are ready to give up their time to cook and serve the meals, if we can raise the funds to provide the food.

"People may think it is unrealistic to imagine something better for the world's poorest children, but I know from seeing Mary's Meals grow it is possible. We're working in the world's poorest communities where so often the poorest children can't go to school because they're working, because they're begging on street corners – doing whatever it takes to put the next meal on the table and therefore they miss out on their education, which is the key to lifting the world's poorest communities out of poverty."

I can't thank you enough for purchasing the book, but my real gratitude is for the donation you have made to this wonderful charity. Please spread the word about Mary's Meals and continue to monitor their fantastic work, checking to see if you can help via www.marysmeals.org.uk and follow them on Twitter for regular updates @MarysMeals

Index

INDEX

Slanj